Praise for Chill

"*Chill* is an intelligent, vulnerable and thought-provoking inquiry on how to give up taking things too personally in life. A book to surely enhance your journey."

Shawne Duperon, 6-Time EMMY® Winner,
Project Forgive Founder

"What Elizabeth Gilbert gave us in *Eat, Pray, Love,* Kara Deringer does in *Chill.* Kara's real and witty sharing is full of wisdom and practical tips. With vulnerability, passion, and spunk, Kara shares personal stories about her life and encourages you to find your own way. This easy to read piece is full of depth and will challenge your thinking. You'll be left wondering when her second book is coming out."

Teresa de Grosbois, 4X #1 Bestselling Author and
International Speaker

Chill

CREATING HAPPINESS IN LIFE AND LOVE

KARA DERINGER

ISBN 978-0-9947987-0-1 paperback
ISBN 978-0-9947987-1-8 eBook

For information about special discounts for bulk purchases,
please contact the publisher:

FLYING COLORS PRESS
info@flyingcolors.ca

Acknowledgments

With the deepest gratitude, thank you to each person who has come into my life. In the perfect way, you have contributed to my life experience and the creation of this book. Thank you to my mother and father who have given me life, invaluable learning, and unconditional love. Thank you to my family and friends who have shared with me their wisdom, encouragement, and love. Thank you to my children for being extraordinary teachers.

Thank you also to those who I have not physically shared time and space with. Thank you to everyone for making this world what it is and what it isn't, which is what has inspired me to write this book. We are all connected. We are beings filled with happiness and love at our core. Let us unleash our essence together.

 *Thank you.*

Contents

Introduction   9

Let It Flow   15

Get Off the Emotional Elephant   51

Honor Your Body as a Temple   77

Give Give Give   107

Go Green   143

Step Over Challenges   169

Get 'Er Done   197

Wonderful Women's Stories   219

Introduction

"Find out who you are and be that person. That's what your soul was put on this Earth to be. Find that truth, live that truth, and everything else will come."

ELLEN DEGENERES

I wrote this book for you. This book is about making a difference in your life. I don't intend to inspire you because inspiration just makes people feel good and tingly inside for a short period of time. I don't intend to inform you because information isn't really what makes the difference—you already know a lot about what theoretically creates happiness. I do intend to incite action. Action is what creates movement and results, which creates a shift. Being inspired and learning more doesn't make a real difference without action. If you've picked up this book, you're open to creating more happiness in life and love. So let's get going and get into action!

Chill is about being more and doing more, with more peace of mind. It isn't about encouraging you to take time to sip mint juleps, walk aimlessly through the park, or get manicures and pedicures. It's about creating happiness and love in your life so that you can then contribute to creating happiness and love in others' lives. Chill is about being present, powerful, and passionate. Chill is about embracing the beauty of being calm, healthy, green (environmentally conscious), generous, and productive.

Somebody asked me if this is a book for the beginners or the advanced. The answer is both. What would make someone advanced, anyway? It doesn't matter whether you call yourself a beginner or advanced. Let's face it: we can all use more happiness and love in our lives. There is always more space inside of us to create an enhanced sense of true inner peace.

Some of us read personal development books, attend seminars, and then wait for results to fall from the sky and into our lives. Some of us complain and whine and expect to get a break one day. Some of us live in a fog and rat race and expect our lives will feel different when circumstances change. Some of us pretend we are okay, and resent other people who seem happier.

Chill is about ending the pretending game that an okay life is good enough. It's about getting out of our bubbles and believing that life is all about us. It's about waking up to recognize that true happiness and love emerges out of contributing to the world around us. It's about recognizing that creating an extraordinary life is entirely possible and absolutely probable with belief, intention, and action.

The message of *Chill* is to look after yourself first and then contribute. Put the oxygen mask on first and be the very best that you can be. With a full cup, you can make a difference for other people—in relationships, in your community, and in the world.

Honestly, the way I see it, nothing in this book is new or revolutionary. What would be new and revolutionary would be for all of us to create a chill life and a chill world. The concepts in this book are simple. We all know that often the simplest things are the hardest to master. These are not new ideas, so I'm leaving it to you to take them on in a new way.

Am I master of all the ideas in this book? No. I'm human. These principles and concepts are ones that I strive to live my life by every day. When I catch myself being stagnant in any area of my life, I reflect on what's preventing me from upping the game. I push myself to look deep and consider who I need to be, and what I need to do, to care for myself and contribute to those around me in a more profound way. There is no end to the depth of love I can feel for myself and others and to the level of happiness that I can create in my life and the lives of others. This journey in growth and learning is limitless.

The most common question I get is, "What inspired you to write the book?" Here's the real truth.

Four years ago, my life looked perfect from the outside. My husband and I had two beautiful kids. We both had good, secure jobs and ample income. We had a lovely home and a nanny. We had good friends and amazing neighbours. But I was unhappy. It seemed like we were in a rat race. We would get up at 6 a.m. and commute from the suburbs to downtown for work. We would get home at 6 p.m. and have an hour and a half to eat and spend time with the kids. The family would go to bed, and I would stay up late to work on my business projects. Then we would get up and do it all over again.

My husband and I had grown apart. Over time it became apparent that we had different values around lifestyle and parenting. His Plan A was for me to be at home full-time with the kids. And if I wasn't going to be a stay-at-home mom, his Plan B was for me to work 9 to 5 in a steady and secure job. But I couldn't bear the idea of giving up my passion and life mission to make a real difference in the world on a big scale, which was not going to fit into either of his two plans. After a number of years of counselling, living apart and together, and even trying to start fresh by dating each other, it was still clear that we are two wonderful, different people who don't mesh and whose visions don't mesh.

The last four years of my life have been extremely full. From engaging in soul searching personal development, to enhancing my relationship with my kids, to growing businesses, to shifting to a healthy lifestyle, to creating new relationships, it has been quite the path. People ask me, "How do you do it all? As a single mom, how do you be with your kids, volunteer, run businesses, stay fit, keep a clean house, spend time with family and friends, and still smile?" I've responded, "That answer is a long one, longer than what we can cover in a coffee conversation. How about I write a book?"

Due to circumstance and timing in my life, a new start began with divorce. By no means do I believe or advocate that this is a requirement for a new start. I don't recommend divorce to anyone who is looking for a segue to reinvent their life. Divorce certainly does not create instant happiness. As the stories of a number of wonderful women in the last chapter of *Chill* illustrate, the choice to create a shift, start anew, and reinvent your life can happen in any given moment and with any circumstances. All it takes is you choosing it.

It is my very strong belief that anyone and everyone can choose a chill life, full of happiness and love, regardless of their life circumstances. Regardless of circumstances, you can make time for fitness, friends, work, etc. It takes creativity, flexibility, and commitment. I have learned to accept the "new normal" of my life and have shifted to make sure that I make time for all of my priorities. I am thankful for my kids' father because when my kids are with him in his home, I know for certain that they are loved to the nth degree, and that they are well fed, learning, and having fun. He is a fabulous father, works hard, and he is kind and generous. His love and care for the kids allows me to work fervently and peacefully when the kids are away, until I am able to be with them again three to five days later. I have shifted to see my life circumstances in a "the glass is half full" manner.

I'm an advocate for people living an exceptional life. I'm an advocate for turning this world around so that our children are surrounded by happy, healthy people. I'm an advocate for taking on a less-is-more approach to life and creating simplicity. I'm an advocate for generosity and contribution. I'm an advocate for a healthy planet.

Most importantly, this book is not mine. It is a creation that has emerged from the wisdom and contribution of many, many, many people. The words in this book are for you, and they come from a whole host of people who believe that we can all find true happiness and love in life. There is much more to share, so I look forward to connecting with you again in the next book.

Let's create a world full of happy and loving people together.

Let It Flow

"Breathe. Let go. And remind yourself that this very moment is the only one you know you have for sure."

OPRAH WINFREY

Life can be exceptional. We should expect exceptional. An exceptional life is created when we focus on our priorities and contributing to others, allow for and look for synchronicities, and let go of trying to control things. When we let it flow moment to moment and day to day, beautiful and rewarding experiences emerge. Life unfolds naturally and exceptionally.

Letting it flow is about balancing two things: having a path and an intention, and letting things unfold naturally. In nature, there is a purpose to everything. One thing connects to another, and the result is absolute perfection. As a river flows toward the ocean, the intention is very clear. The path deviates, with the water flowing over rocks, and sometimes flowing around them. It is important to have goals and plans (as the water intends to reach the ocean), but when we are stuck and fixed on plans and goals, we don't let the universe take care of things naturally. Sometimes what seem like obstacles (rocks) in the moment are actually part of a perfect path unfolding. When we let things unfold naturally, a chain of events and outcomes can emerge that are even better than we planned or expected.

Don't Bob Along

It's not an accident that as I began writing this chapter in a coffee shop, a man and woman having a conversation beside me caught my attention. Based on the body language and conversation of the two, it seemed that they were casual friends. The 260-pound man, who was wearing jeans and a NYPD navy ball cap, was unusually positive and loud. A number of the things he was saying were fitting for this chapter. As I heard him saying the following phrases, I smiled and was grateful for the synchronicity. He spoke to the woman across from him, and said the following:

- "Oh, don't worry about it."

- "When I'm tired, I get thinking differently. Yes, that's a nice way to put it. I think differently."

- "I just like to let go of the argument route. It's okay to be wrong."

This man had the perfect message for this chapter. Number one: don't worry. Worrying and fussing takes a lot of energy and gets in the way of being present to the perfection of the here and now. Number two: when you're tired, your ability to let it flow is reduced. When you take care of yourself—when you are rested and healthy—you can think more clearly, be intentional, and also be relaxed and go with the flow. Number three: let go of needing to be in control and right. When we set our ego aside, we have less of a need to be defensive, right, and controlling; we can let people and situations be for how they are and how they are not.

After some casual conversation, the man's lady friend got up to go to the washroom, and he turned to me and said, "It's busy in here today." I smiled politely. He said, "She works at Memorial Hospital. We just run into each other here sometimes, and then we have coffee. I don't even have her phone number." I responded, "Hmm. So you just run into each other when it's meant to be." "I guess so," he said. The man and I introduced ourselves. His name is Bob. Bob began talking about a trip to New York that he had taken—it wasn't clear if the trip happened a month, or a decade, prior. Regardless of when Bob's big adventure was, he spoke of the trip to New York like it was yesterday.

After a few minutes of New York chatter, we got back to talking about Bob's lady friend. He said, "We just have coffee. That's all I need. I just want a coffee friend. I like my alone time." I smiled somewhat mischievously. With warm eyes, I said to Bob, "That's what a lot of people say—that they would rather be on their own." Bob went on to justify why he is better off alone, explained how long he's been on his own, and concluded why he only needs a coffee friend. With another smile I said, "Maybe it's time to step out of your comfort zone." Bob smiled slightly, perhaps a little mischievously himself this time. There was a hint of recognition in what I was suggesting.

Bob was the perfect illustration of what I wanted to write about on the topic of "let it flow." He represents the incongruity of how we see ourselves and how we want to be—versus who we actually are. Bob seemed to perceive himself as having a laissez faire approach to life and an easygoing personality with an adventurous side. Yet Bob appeared to have a huge block in the way of letting true happiness and love flow into his life. While Bob talked the talk, he didn't completely walk the walk. Truly letting it flow would look like welcoming love into his life, rather than justifying being alone. Bob was limited in his thinking in how happy he could be, which completely contradicted his persona of an easygoing kind of guy. In true "let it flow" style, Bob would be as open to the unfolding of an adventure with his lady friend as he was to creating his adventures in New York.

The point of the story is that many of us are just bobbing along in life, staying afloat and moving naturally as the water flow of life carries us along. We are not creating powerful intentions in the path of our own lives. We are limited in our ability to believe and imagine that life can be exceptional, and we do not allow for the path of life to take us in incredible directions. Life is only ever good, fine, or okay.

There's a difference in being easygoing, being at the effect of life, and settling for an okay existence—versus letting it flow. The latter requires trusting in the infinite abundance of possibilities in life and being excited about unfolding miracles while also being at peace with how life is in the present. It is an art of believing in abundance and living in acceptance. What seems like challenge and imperfection needs to be accepted, but not as stagnant (how things are meant to be or will continue to be). How things are can be accepted for how things are in the present with the intention of continuing to create an abundant and exceptional life going forward. (Go to www.karaderinger.com and register now for a coaching program to assist you in creating an exceptional life.)

Set a Foundation

When I let go and let things flow, I am amazed at how easily and quickly things happen in my life. It is as if a natural force takes over and takes care of things. This happens on a daily basis because I am committed to living life based on these foundations:

• Health—When I start to feel tired, annoyed, worried, stressed, judgmental, testy, anxious, etc., I look at what is missing in my life in the way of wellness, whether it be water, exercise, sleep, vitamins, fresh air, fruits and vegetables, social time, or something else. I know that my ability to let it flow is highly dependent on me being vital, grounded, connected, and relaxed.

• KISS (keeping it super simple)—When anything starts to feel difficult and when things are not falling into place, I question why I'm pursuing it. Perhaps I'm doing it because I think I should, because I have a fixed idea about how things should go, or otherwise. When I stop pushing and forcing, let go, and either look for an easier way or just allow things to sort themselves out, things often get simple naturally.

• Purpose—When I am connected to my purpose—that the reason I am on this planet is to make a difference and to empower women—the little things and my perceived challenges seem insignificant compared to the bigger picture. I can ground myself by looking at how my current experiences are contributing to my learning and growth and how this will support me in what I'm meant to accomplish and contribute in this world.

In order to generate flow, the universe needs to know what direction we are headed in and what our desired path is. When we are clear about how we are committed to make a difference in the world, we can set intentions and allow people and experiences to flow into our lives to support this. The universe will be far more generous in supporting the creation of wealth when it is for a higher purpose, such as building playgrounds or libraries, creating a scholarship, planting trees, feeding the poor, forming a charity, or another worthy endeavor.

When we care for our well-being, focus on simplicity, and create intentions around our higher purpose, life flows beautifully. Rather than feeling worn down, stewing over roadblocks, and complaining about how unsatisfying life is, every day we can make choices to ensure that our foundation is set for letting things flow and experiencing an exceptional life.

What do you see as missing in your ability to let it flow?

_____

_____

_____

_____

What are you committed to shift in your foundation in order to let it flow?

_____

_____

_____

_____

_____

_____

_____

See What Flow Looks Like

What does flow look like on a daily basis? It is absolutely wonderful! Day-to-day flow generates an abundance of opportunities and results. Life unfolds in a way that is far easier and far more fulfilling than you could even imagine. Here are some personal stories that illustrate flow that I have experienced.

The Top

On a Sunday, when I had committed to myself that I would spend the afternoon writing, I found a popular brand-name top on an online used site that I wanted to buy. When I inquired via text if the top was still available, the seller said that it was and that she lived on the north side of the city. The trip would be about a 45-minute drive for me.

With online classified ad buying and selling, my main rule is to KISS, as is my rule with other things in life. I asked the lady if she travels to other parts of the city and shared that I would be downtown in two days (which is about 60–70 percent closer to her area of the city than my neighborhood). She responded by saying that her two little ones (1.5 and 3 years old) were sick that day and that she was planning to drive around the city mid-day that day anyway to put them to sleep. She said she may as well drive somewhere in particular rather than drive in circles. She said that she would be happy to drop the top off. An hour later, she arrived in my driveway with her two little ones in the car. I ran out the front door, gave her the money for the top, and away she went. This was perfect synchronicity.

The Renters

Two gentlemen were renting a suite from me that was less than a year old with high-end finishings. I had marketed the suite as a furnished, executive property. When the renters began renting, they expressed disappointment that some of the things they were expecting in a furnished unit weren't there, including a toaster oven, coffee maker, comfortable bed sheets, blender, and trash can. I explained to them that different people have different expectations of what furnished means and that the previous tenants hadn't complained. In fact, some past tenants had brought their own favorite house gadgets such as a coffee maker or iron because they liked particular brands or types. Nonetheless, I agreed to supply all of these items to the tenants, placing importance on building trust and my relationship with them. In return, I asked that they keep the unit very clean and in executive condition.

When I visited the unit a few months later for a trade repair appointment, I found that the unit wasn't clean. The renters weren't present for me to talk to, so I phoned them later to ask that they clean up. They declined, stating that it was their right to live as they chose to. In this phone conversation, I thanked the renter for his time and said calmly, "So you're declining my request to clean." He confirmed.

I considered evicting the renters but had a gut feeling that would create unwanted negative energy and drama. I chose to write a note to the universe asking for exactly what I wanted— namely that the renters would choose to leave peacefully and respectfully of their own will in short time. My request looked like this:

Name and name:

- offer to leave graciously;

- continue to care for the home—quiet, clean and damage free;

- find a wonderful new place to live in quickly and easily;

- pay all rent and utilities on time and in full; and

- leave the home on time, clean, and free of damage, with all furnishings, equipment, and accessories intact.

A month later, the tenants paid their last month's rent and gave their one month's notice. They said that I was welcome to show the unit to potential new renters at any time. They left the unit reasonably clean, with all furnished items intact, and with little damage.

The Pad Thai

As I was writing this chapter, I took a break from writing one afternoon and walked down the street to find some lunch. I passed a couple of sales people standing on the sidewalk in front of a restaurant who asked me if I wanted some free Pad Thai. I was especially hungry, as I had just spent two hours past my lunchtime writing. I said, "Sure, I'd like some free Pad Thai." Like most would, I was wondering what the catch was. They explained to me that I needed to download their company's ordering and delivery app for takeout food on my phone. Then we would order my free Pad Thai using my new app, and I could go inside to pick it up. "Fair enough," I thought. I downloaded the app and about eight minutes later I had my free Pad Thai. Just like that. Easy-peasy.

The Vase

I had been looking for a pair of very large outdoor vases to place on each side of my driveway. I had looked in many home décor stores and home improvement stores, but had not found the size, color, and material I was looking for. I had a strong sense of what I was looking for, even though I hadn't actually seen anything of the sort around town or in advertisements. Finally, one day, I walked into a chain décor store that I had never been inside of and saw my dream outdoor vase. There it was! Wow! They had one vase, and it was 50 percent off. I put the vase on hold, as I couldn't fit it in my car that day. When I went to pick up the vase a few days later at the store, it had been marked down to 75 percent off. I was thrilled. I asked if they had another vase, but they didn't. They encouraged me to call the toll-free number for their headquarters to ask about the availability in local stores.

I called headquarters and was told they didn't have any more of these vases left in the entire province—not in the city 1.5 hours away and not in the city three hours away, both of which where I have friends who could easily pick it up for me. They did have a vase in British Columbia (B.C.), the neighboring province. I called the store in B.C. and asked if they would ship the vase to our store here. They said they couldn't. I asked if I could pay for the vase and arrange for the shipping myself. They said they couldn't do that either because they don't accept payment over the phone. I was puzzled with this lack of service and the lack of options given the size of the retail chain. I asked a girlfriend who lives in B.C. if she would be willing to pick up the vase, but she said the retail store was well out of her way and she was concerned about picking up a vase of that size and weight. At this point, I was reminded of my mantra to keep things super simple and was starting to think I was taking this vase acquisition mission too far.

As a final attempt before letting the vase go, I contacted my aunt who lives in a small island community in B.C. but often works in the city. She said that she would not be working in the city in the next few days, but that her friend's daughter actually lives in the area of the store. She called the daughter to see if she would be willing to pick up the vase. (My aunt admitted later that she was also questioning the logic of my persistence in trying to purchase this vase.) The daughter was incidentally headed to that exact shopping area that afternoon. She happily agreed to pick up the vase, pay for it, and accept payment from me to reimburse her. My aunt said that she would pick up the vase from the daughter, as she was long overdue to meet the daughter's newest baby (who was no longer a baby). It all worked out. My aunt picked up the vase from the daughter and ended up driving the vase to me (a 12-hour drive) months later when she was driving my cousin back home and picking up some personal items for herself to take home to B.C.

The Job

My first "real" job coming out of my graduate degree program was working for the federal government in a policing department. I was hired as an internal conflict management practitioner, which means that when there was conflict between a manager and an employee or two co-workers or in a team, I would be called in to assist the individuals in resolving their differences. It is far more cost effective for large government departments to have a conflict management practitioner (professional mediator, facilitator, and trainer) on staff than to contract these services out.

I took the job for the financial security, benefits, and work experience. I wanted to build my own consulting practice, but my husband at the time and I decided that taking the job was the wise move to make. Over the next several years, I worked for the policing department, took a maternity leave, returned to work with the policing department, took another maternity leave, and then returned to work with the health department in the federal government.

Over time, I became worn down with work. I was dealing with workplace conflict full-time, which was emotionally exhausting. I was also travelling out of town up to 50 percent of the time, leaving two little ones at home. When our children were one and three, I shared with my husband that I wanted to be home more with the kids, do consulting work, and create more of a work-life balance. From a financial perspective, I pointed out that we would save money on child care, which would ease the pressure of me creating a replacement income with the consulting work. From an emotional perspective, we could create quality time for the kids and our relationship. But he was not supportive of me pursuing entrepreneurial endeavors.

About a year later, when my husband and I parted ways, I also chose to leave my government position. This was a bold move. I was becoming a single mom and moving into full-on entrepreneurship all in one shot. It was quickly apparent that working in my business and being at home part-time was the beautiful balance that I imagined it would be. I nurtured a number of business projects and was busy and fulfilled in continuing to build my career. I had time to eat well, exercise, play with the kids, take the kids to activities, do play dates with family friends, and deal with the logistics and responsibilities of life, which included moving through divorce-related meetings and legalities, as well as moving homes four times over at the time.

Although I was fairly certain that I would never return to government when I left my government position, after two years of focusing on building my business, I began thinking about going back to work. My daughter would be entering kindergarten six months later, so I could see new work hours opening up in the days. The writing of this book was nearing completion. One day, I found myself talking to a colleague and discovered that the policing department that I'd worked with previously had a position open. Not only that, but it was managed by my former manager, who was an excellent manager and had become a close friend of mine since I'd worked with him eight years prior. My thoughts were on going back to work, and now there was a fairly easy back-to-work option.

Things were flowing, but I could feel resistance in me. I asked myself whether this was head resistance or gut resistance. Was there ego at play that didn't want my ex-husband to think that I wasn't successful in business, which wasn't true? Was it that I was worried about going backward? Or was it that I feared the job would suck my energy and take away from me focusing on being an author, coach, and trainer? Was it that taking the job didn't feel like the right next step given my passion and commitment to make a real difference on this planet?

I chose to trust that life was flowing in this direction for a reason. I chose to get over my ego of fearing judgment from my former husband and from myself for taking a step backward. I chose not to see it as a step backward because going back to work would fulfill my short-term need for financial security in order to continue on my long-term path of fulfilling my purpose in life. I let my manager friend know that I was interested in going back to work. I was honest with him and shared that my intention was to work for a relatively short period of time.

I asked the policing department for a part-time work and travel schedule, with the option of working from home. They said yes, and even came back offering me fewer hours so that I didn't have to work from home on my mommy days. Everything was falling into place. I'd still be working part-time and be at home with the kids part-time. I could still walk the kids to school and pick them up from school. There was no need to arrange child care. On my mommy days, while the kids would be in school, I would have the mornings to work on my business. I could see that going back to work would actually free up energy. It would give me a stable income to ensure the kids' needs were cared for rather than stressing about generating new business every month. This would provide me with the financial stability and peace of mind to focus my energy on moving my career in a new and exciting direction. Everything was flowing. And the decision to go back to work was in line with my higher purpose.

See What Flow Isn't

Letting it flow doesn't mean sitting back, twiddling our thumbs, and expecting our needs to be magically met. It doesn't mean waiting for challenges to magically disappear. It doesn't mean simply doing what we think other people want. It doesn't mean expecting other people to read our minds and biting our tongues from stating our preferences. We need to take action in our life and communicate with and connect to people. Flow is about powerfully balancing being proactive with being laissez-faire.

There is a balance between hard work and persistence and letting it flow. You need to take action but then sometimes back off to allow things to fall into place. If things don't fall into place, then decide whether to take another action or let it go. We can strengthen our ability to constantly consider what is happening naturally and what we are working too hard for. Only you can decide if the hard work is necessary or if you are creating hard work and pushing in an unnatural way.

Going with the flow doesn't mean that you get to jam out of hard work all the time. Life can be flowing and things can seem easy or hard. I know some people who, when something doesn't fall from the sky and into their laps, simply say, "Oh well...it wasn't meant to be." As soon as something becomes hard, they decide that it isn't for them and that it's not synchronistic. There are some things that are simply hard. For example, successfully completing the theoretical and practical requirements of medical school is hard. It takes effort and dedication.

There is a fine line between copping out and letting it flow. You are the only one who knows when you are copping out. You may choose not to take an action or go down a path, but you need to test for yourself if you're letting it flow or copping out. Someone else may challenge you to look at whether you're copping out, but only you know the real truth. It takes real courage and authenticity to admit when you are copping out. Don't make the mistake of thinking that letting it flow means copping out.

My belief is that the universe tests us. As we overcome challenges, we're demonstrating our capacity and strength. If we desire extraordinary amounts of resources and success in our life, we need to demonstrate our extraordinary ability to deal with the accompanying challenges. We need to be up for taking on hard work and not copping out, while also being masterful at letting go of plans when they are not flowing.

Going with the flow does not mean accommodating everyone's wishes or expecting them to accommodate ours. If you're wishy-washy and expect things to fall from the sky, you're going to end up being at the effect of life and not in flow. If you don't state your preferences, remain in touch with your values, and make boundaries, you're going to end up feeling like a doormat. This isn't a step in the right direction of creating positive energy. We keep talking about balance. It's important to balance being clear and expressive about preferences and also being flexible and accepting with what's happening.

On the day of my encounter with Bob in the coffee shop, my partner and I got into an argument. We were visiting and staying with friends of his in another city at the time, and that morning these friends had mentioned that they were planning to go out to see a garden that night. I had shared with my partner on our walk that morning that I wasn't up for going to the garden. Apparently he hadn't heard or understood my preference because, later that day, he was making plans with his friends for us to go to the garden.

I asked him if we could speak privately. He wanted to know why I didn't want to go to the garden. I shared that my preference was for us to spend time alone, since that was our primary intention for going away and not something we often have the opportunity to do. I was surprised to hear his viewpoint. He said that we were visiting a beautiful city and that it made sense to get out and do things that we couldn't do at home. He thought we would grow our relationship by spending time getting to know each others' friends. I was surprised to hear him say he would rather go out with friends because he had been so keen to take a vacation in order to have alone time. We obviously had different ideas about how much alone time to have and what kind of alone time that would be. I became upset and said, "I just don't want to."

He told the friends that we would pass on seeing the garden and that we were going to go out for dinner. At dinner, I shared with my partner that I had been writing about "letting it flow" that afternoon. We both laughed at the irony.

After dinner, we headed back to the friends' house. The family was out at the garden so we had the place to ourselves. We began talking and my partner asked what was really going on. I said that I didn't know. I couldn't put my finger on it. I still didn't know why our disagreement about going to the garden upset me so much. He persisted and urged me to try and put words to what I was feeling and thinking. I began talking. (Although I like to be logical and articulate in my thoughts and feelings, I've learned that when I don't have myself figured out, I need to push myself to dump the nonsense out of my head and heart in order to explore and make sense of what's actually going on for me.)

Over an hour of conversation, and me dumping, we discovered that what was actually at the root of my upset was that my values of respect and privacy were being challenged. We had stayed with two families on our trip at that point and because it was the holiday season, they also had family staying with them. I was concerned that we were intruding on their family holiday time. The houses were full. Intimate sounds can travel, and with homes filled with family members, I wanted to be respectful as a guest, but I also wanted to enjoy intimacy on our vacation.

I share this story because I think it needs to be clear that letting it flow doesn't always mean getting over whatever's going on. When we ignore and silence our thoughts and emotions, our space is full of anxiety, frustration, stress, worry, disappointment, etc. There is no room for real flow to occur in life because we're overflowing with chatter from our inner voice and tension from our body. It is critical to give voice to the thoughts and feelings bubbling inside of us in order to move through the situation and let it go in order to move forward. Giving voice to these thoughts and emotions can be done in a gentle, loving, and respectful way without drama and turmoil.

It also needs to be said that letting it flow doesn't mean compromising your values. When you're upset in any way, something to look at is what might be touching on your values. What you need at your core and what you believe to be right and wrong will rub you the wrong way no matter which way you look at it. Values need to be communicated with the people in your life so that they can be acknowledged. In the case of our vacation, I was reminded of my values of paying respect to people when staying in their home and having privacy as a couple.

I'm certainly not recommending that every time that you're upset or don't want to do something that you simply look for a value that is being challenged to justify why you're upset or don't want to do something. When we identify and discuss the values at the root of a situation, we can come up with some ideas on how to make sure our values are honored so that we can create some steps for moving forward that are in flow and also in line with our values.

Listen to Messages

I was sitting in a coffee shop one day debating whether to write for another hour or walk home to write there. I heard a message, "Walk home. It's going to rain shortly." I packed up my things to walk home. Sure enough, as I was arriving home, it started to rain. Was this a thought or a message? Was it a coincidence or synchronicity?

Have you had experiences where the same names or places or other messages kept popping into conversations, images, your thoughts, etc.? There are no accidents. Whatever you want to call this—intuition, higher power, gut feelings, angels, sixth sense—it's a very powerful force that will support you in staying in flow if you are open to the messages.

As I was about halfway done writing this book, and as people in my life were asking about my progress on it, a number of people suggested that it's good to go away from home to write in order to really get in the zone. Someone in my mastermind group asked me what distracts me. I said that I work from home so there are always chores and other business tasks to get done. He made the suggestion that I drive to another city to spend a weekend writing.

A few weeks later, my aunt mentioned that she had an airline credit that was expiring soon and that it could only be transferred to a family member. The flight needed to be booked in the next month. I had a sense that the airline credit was meant for me, but I couldn't figure out where I was meant to go. There was a professional retreat in Hawaii that I had considered attending, but I wasn't 100 percent drawn to the retreat. I didn't have any upcoming business or personal events that required travel. I was pondering and pondering the reason I was receiving the message about the airline credit...and then it occurred to me.

When my ex-husband asked whether I wanted to stay with our original plan of him being with the kids over the Easter weekend for five days or if I would I like to shift the plan and be with them over the five-day weekend, everything clicked. I wanted to be with the kids over Easter, no doubt. Doing egg hunts, eating chocolate, riding bikes, and playing games would all be absolutely amazing. At the same time, a small window to complete the book was wide open. I had my friends' encouragement to get away to write. I had the opportunity to buy the airline credit. And I had the time. Plus I had committed to going back to work part-time in the near future, which meant that now was the best time to finish the book. Everything was flowing, and the messages were clear.

The key is to practice noticing messages, inquire into their meaning, and take action. There are no right or wrong choices, but the universe works to open our eyes to new opportunities and pathways that we may not have thought of so that we have the chance to move in these directions. When we're open to the messages, we can also inquire into their meaning. For instance, the name of a person may keep coming up, but it may not be clear why or how this person fits. It is important to remain open to messages that bring to light possible next steps related to this person.

Sometimes the message is fairly clear but the timing isn't. For instance, there was a period of about six months where every few weeks a colleague would mention a trainer and business person in the community who they said I should meet. When they would say the new contact's name, I would think, "Hmm, there's his name again." One of the first colleagues who mentioned his name actually introduced the two of us via email. Because the new contact person is busy, and neither of us was clear about how we fit together, the email introduction fell flat. A number of months later, it occurred to me to ask this person to be a speaker at our city's Holistic Chamber of Commerce meeting, of which I am the President. He accepted. He was the right person to connect with in so many ways, but six months earlier, when his name first started emerging in messages, wasn't the right time.

We all have a strong sense of intuition, but most of us choose to block it out most of the time. We talk about funny coincidences and hunches and gut feelings, but we don't allow our intuition to guide us on a moment-to-moment basis. We are grateful for the synchronicities that put us in the right place at the right time, especially if it gives us something like more money. However, we are not practiced in seeking messages to guide our choices. (And I mean seeking, not passively noticing messages but actively looking for them.) Being open—truly open—to messages is a practice and an art.

Acknowledge Your Own Flow

The more we acknowledge flow in our lives and the more we are grateful for the flow, the more space we create for flow to happen more often and in bigger ways. This practice of observing and appreciating flow is one that we can strengthen every day. Here are some signs of flow:

- You write on your to-do list that you need to contact someone, and a few hours later they initiate communication with you.

- You decide you need an item, and it turns up shortly thereafter at a convenient place and price (sometimes free).

- You create a list of characteristics that you are looking for in a new job and a friend mentions a position open in their organization that fits your wish list perfectly.

- You run into someone you know and find out that they are having a super tough day; s/he needs a hug and a heart-to-heart chat.

- You need to spend an extra 10 minutes at work, but because you stayed, you avoid a backlog of traffic from a train crossing; it clears up just as you are approaching the area.

• You bump into the person you have been playing phone tag with at the grocery store.

• You're looking for a service and someone you know mentions in passing this same service that they use and love.

• You need a ride somewhere and overhear someone talking about heading out to the same area.

• You paste a picture of a sustainably built vacation home on your goal board and a nearly identical vacation home in your budget comes up for sale near your family's property.

• You are thinking fondly of someone and they call or text you.

• You can't buy an item because it's out of stock, but you find the same item at another store at a lower price, or a different item that is better quality and/or a better fit.

What flow have you experienced recently?

_____

_____

_____

_____

    One holiday evening, I shared with my uncle that I wanted to purchase a Himalayan salt lamp for the house. He jumped out of his chair, went into the bedroom, and came out with a beautiful, round salt lamp in his hands. He said, "I was just thinking the other day that I should give this away to someone who would appreciate it. Here you go!

Chill 36

I had been intending for some time to find some clear plastic earring support backs, and it had been on my to-do list for weeks. I had visited two fashion jewelry stores to look for the earring backs and the sales people had no idea what I was looking for. In the spirit of flow, I decided not to push forward in finding them. I was waiting for the perfect flow moment to easily discover and buy the earring backs.

One night, while working and reviewing my to-do list, I decided to tackle the earring backs and quickly looked on eBay for them. Sure enough, I found some. The ad read "RARE EARRING BACKS." Apparently they were "rare." The problem was, the seller only shipped to the United States. I tapped my brain to think of someone I knew living in the U.S. or with a U.S. postal address, but couldn't think of anyone. The next day, when exchanging Facebook messages with a lady interested in buying some items from me, she asked if I would be shipping to Canada or the U.S. because she has both a Canadian and U.S. mailing address. Bingo! I arranged to ship her items to her Canadian address. Then, I explained the eBay earring back situation to her and asked if she would be willing to accept the earring backs at her U.S. address and forward them to me in Canada. She happily agreed. I gave her a discount on her items to thank her. At the end of the day, rather than spending an hour or two looking in retail stores for the earring backs, I had that time to be with my kids instead.

Flow can happen all day every day if we believe in it and allow for it, but many of us talk ourselves out of letting it flow. For whatever reason, we have an expectation that life needs to be difficult and dramatic. Rather than expecting events to easily unfold every day, we become stressed in thinking that we are going to have to work hard or even fight for what we think we want and deserve. Rather than giving space and time for things to work themselves out, we become pushy and controlling and try to make things happen in our own way and in our own time. Rather than being accepting and grateful for wonderful people and events, we make out like we don't deserve for flow to happen or that we feel guilty for flow having happened. Stop pushing away flow. Start acknowledging, accepting, and welcoming flow.

Being in flow is about being calm and at peace with whatever is going on, whether the events that occur are positive or negative. What seems negative in the moment (whether small or big) can be a stepping stone to something amazing. I know this sounds cliché, and I know that you've probably heard it before. What would be new would be taking on an openness and commitment to look for the gift in everything that we experience every day rather than complaining and wishing for something else. This is so much easier said than done.

One day when leaving the house, our overhead garage door wouldn't close. The kids and I needed to zip across town to drop off my son with my mom and get my daughter to her dance lesson. Without getting upset, I got out of the car, unplugged the electrical system for the overhead garage door control panel, and pulled the overhead door down manually. Ten minutes later, a friend texted me to ask if she could drop off a box of items at the house that she had been meaning to bring by for some time. I said that today was the perfect day because she could come by anytime, lift the overhead door, and slide the box under the garage door!

It's good practice to check in with yourself on an ongoing basis to determine the extent to which you are letting things flow in life. Our openness to let it flow can change on an hour-to-hour, day-to-day and week-to-week basis. We can move in and out of letting it flow. When you're feeling resentful, disappointed, or frustrated about something, first go ahead and acknowledge the emotion. (After all, we're only human.) Then check in with yourself on how you thought things should be or go. Compare your expectations/ideal/story with what's actually happening or not happening. Look for something to be grateful for in how things are in reality. Then take a step that is in line with your goals and plans. That's it. Our openness to flow can change in a moment if we continually commit to getting ourselves back in flow.

On a scale from 1 to 10, how much would you say your life is flowing right now? How come?

_____

_____

_____

_____

_____

_____

_____

Speak Exceptionally

The more we tell ourselves mentally and tell others verbally through our words that everything is perfect and that the journey we are on is perfect, the more we put this positive and accepting energy out there—and believe in it. Perfect doesn't always mean that things are easy or fun. It means that we can see that things are unfolding in a natural order. We can see that we are learning and growing through our challenges, and that in the big picture, we are creating a life full of happiness and love. We don't need to be artificially positive and pretend that all of life is wonderful always. We can speak about the challenges we're experiencing authentically and share the steps we're taking to overcome the challenges, the things that have been happening in perfect synchronicity, and how we are on our path of fulfilling our purpose and intentions.

This means getting out of the habit of being negative and okay in what we say to ourselves and others and getting into the habit of being positive and exceptional. Let's move away from complaining, gossiping, and storytelling. Let's move away from focusing on the "ho-hum" of life and focus on what's exciting and extraordinary. We get into patterns of communication where we're numb to how negative and ordinary our language and conversations are, which sets us up to feel a low level of energy. We do this out of habit and without knowing it.

Take on a commitment to develop a revitalized vocabulary and a renewed approach to conversations that interrupts the negative and mundane energy and that generates an enthusiastic and passionate view of life. On a scale of 1 to 10 in terms of energy and positivity, 1 would be terrible, 5 would be okay, and 10 would be exceptional. We want to focus on feeling and believing and talking about how we are in that 8–10 range in our life. The 8–10 range is in the space of "Oooh baby!" For example:

Question	Oooh baby! Response
How are you?	Unbelievable!
You look great! How do you do it?	Thank you! I've been...
How's the weather?	This morning was so, so sunny!
How are things?	Life is rockin'!

Chill 40

Question	Oooh baby! Response
How is your day going?	Couldn't be better!
How is work?	I had a great conversation...
What's new?	Nothing but good things!
How is (person)?	S/he is so happy!
How did it go yesterday?	It was incredible because...
What are you up to these days?	You know, I'm so grateful for...

Of course, this is just the start of the conversation. But by starting your response with optimism and enthusiasm, you're now setting yourself up to have a conversation about the happiness and love in your life rather than the woes and tragedies. Now the volume, tone, and level of enthusiasm makes all the difference in these "Oooh baby!" responses. Even if you do need to do some acting and up the positivity in the first part of your response to generate energy, go ahead and do it in order to create some momentum. Once you respond with something different than your usual, mundane reply, you'll be surprised with what authentically flows from you after that. Just let it flow and let it happen naturally.

One night my partner asked me, "Have you ever noticed that women sit around having coffee and lunch, talking about their problems? They all talk about what's wrong and what they're dealing with. And the woman with the biggest problem wins. They leave the coffee shop having complained about their lives and think that was quality time spent with friends."

Try the following experiment: sit in a coffee shop or restaurant or walk down the street and notice the conversations around you. Notice the people who are talking about their hardships and the intolerable jerks in their lives. Notice the people who are talking about the weather and the mundane, ho-hum goings on in their lives. Notice the people who are talking about their accomplishments and possessions. Notice the people who are complaining about the decisions of decision-makers. Notice the people who are talking about other people. Get present to the energy of these conversations and the effect on you even just in hearing them.

We can shift our ability to acknowledge and attract flow simply in the way we talk. Catch yourself talking about your complaints, judgments, heartaches, and apathy. When you start, stop yourself. Start having conversations about what you're learning about yourself, your amazing family and friends, your goals and plans, your amazing life. Yes, you may share the hurdles and obstacles, but share them in the context of what you're working to overcome or what you're grateful for, and how you're learning and growing along the way. This is a completely different conversation, which celebrates and invites flow into your life.

Be Trusting

There can be a tendency to worry and believe that people are going to hurt us, steal from us, let us down, abandon us, damage our things, etc. This is a human condition. We're wired this way to protect ourselves. When we let this orientation to people and life run us, we end up being suspicious, cautious, cold, solitary, stingy, protective, disconnected, and accusational.

When we have a commitment to see people as having good hearts and good intentions and as being honest, generous, and trustworthy, we commit to see and operate in the world in a trusting way. The world becomes a safe and giving place where we can experience happiness and love wherever we go and in whatever we do.

When I choose to see the world in this way, this is my experience more often than not. Things that other people complain about—like stealing, rudeness, backstabbing, etc.—aren't things that I experience often. (And if they do happen, I simply see them as something that happened and don't let the events or stories about the events consume me.)

Often when I'm selling a used item in the online classifieds, I'll leave it on my porch for the buyer to come pick up at their leisure. I simply ask the buyer to put the money under the doormat. I don't expect people to take the item without leaving payment because I live in a world of trust. Sometimes I'm out of town when they pick up the item, so the item sits on my porch for a few days and then the money sits under the mat for a few days. Only once in hundreds of transactions did one person take something from the porch without leaving money.

Rather than spending precious time marking our family's belongings with our name to ensure they stay in our possession, we pay attention to keeping track of our things and trust that others won't take them. This gives us more time and energy to enjoy being together. I heard once from a spiritual teacher that the more attached you are to a material possession, the more likely you are to lose it. I believe this. I choose to trust that what is meant to remain ours will remain ours. In fact, at a deeper level, nothing is ours anyway—since we're all connected to each other and the universe, what's mine is actually yours, which is the universe.

Anytime I catch myself worrying about being wronged, I make the choice to trust and let go and recreate my world as one where people are loving, generous, and honest. The more I do this, the more I'm proven right that trusting and letting go was the right thing to do.

Start to identify any negative and limiting beliefs that come from your upbringing that aren't necessarily yours at their roots and that limit you from being trusting. Family stories of hardship, tragedy, suffering, mistreatment, etc. can create a lack of trust when it's not needed. Sometimes the stories may be of experiences that you were a part of, but other times they may be stories that were just passed down.

Let the fear and caution go. Trust that things happen for a reason. There are no accidents. Trusting that everything is unfolding perfectly and as it should gives a sense of peace and acceptance with how things are. Every person we encounter, every experience that occurs...it all unfolds with perfection. Even when it doesn't feel perfect to us, each moment is an opportunity for us to seek the perfection in what may seem imperfect. We can look at what we're learning and remind ourselves of our higher intentions and purpose. This approach to life requires patience, acceptance, and trust.

Being trusting is not necessarily something that will emerge and drive you after reading this section; it's a continual choice and commitment. In order to get present to how being trusting can make a positive difference in your life, start to notice how being trusting frees up your time and energy. Notice how events begin to unfold beautifully as you trust and believe that people are good. If you commit to believing in and trusting the good and abundance in the world, you may just prove yourself right that the world is good and abundant!

What prevents you from being trusting?

_____

_____

_____

_____

_____

How are you committed to be more trusting?

_____

_____

_____

_____

_____

_____

Believe You Can Have It All

I remember one of my personal development course leaders saying with deep passion and conviction, "You can have it all! You just need to believe it and create it. Don't try to do it alone, though. You can have it all if you allow for the people around you to contribute to you having it all." I see now that for many years I was getting in the way of myself having it all because I hadn't really committed to believing it could happen and making it happen. I mean really committed.

It can be a real challenge to continue committing to having it all when things seem like they're slipping sideways or, worse yet, when it seems like we're sitting at the bottom of a deep, dark hole. When good things are happening and everything is flowing, it seems entirely possible to have it all. It's a positive, light, and abundant energy that seems to grow and build on itself naturally. The challenge is to maintain that deep belief in and commitment to happiness, abundance, love, and contribution even in the foggy, gloomy, or stormy times.

The challenge that I created for myself was to learn to live in flow and to commit to having it all. My intention was to become a person who had the internal capacity to be at peace with anything and anyone. Regardless of the challenges that were occurring in my life, I wanted to be a person that remained steady, positive, grounded, and committed to my life being full of happiness and love. My good friend and colleague Vik Maraj asked me one day, "What would it be like to never get upset Kara? Like no matter what anyone says, and no matter what happens, you don't get upset." I admitted that I couldn't even imagine what it would be like to stay in power in life and not be at the effect of the people and events around me. That was a turning point for me in choosing to take on this challenge.

I'm still learning and growing inside of this challenge to create and have it all, but I can certainly acknowledge that I've created transformation in my life in the last few years. One day a few months ago, while talking to a colleague, he asked how I was doing. I said, "Living the dream." He laughed and said, "People say that sarcastically, Kara. How are you really?" I laughed and replied, "That's funny. No really, I'm living the dream." In that moment, I was reflecting on how many heavy-hearted coffee conversations my colleague and I had shared in past years as I was struggling with work, kids, and marriage. But I had completely turned my life around and had created a dream life. I had taken on transforming one area of my life at a time—kids, work, health, family, friends, and partnership. I was living my dream life being at home half-time with my kids and working on my businesses half-time. I was the healthiest I had ever been in terms of both fitness and diet. I was spending lots of time with family and friends. And I was creating a new partnership.

I remember my ex-husband saying to me one day, "You can't have it all, Kara. You need to make some choices." That was a defining moment in our relationship for me. I remember seriously questioning whether I was crazy to think that I could have it all and then coming back to my firm belief that it takes commitment and creativity to have it all in life. When he said, "You can't have it all," I saw more clearly in that moment than I had before that the two of us had fundamentally different approaches and beliefs about how life works and what's possible.

When it doesn't seem like an event—or life in general—is exceptional, an enhanced level of being patient, accepting, and trusting is required in order to put one foot in front of the other and believe that the learning and strength that will come from the experience will be beautiful and rewarding. Even through the dark days or weeks, it's so important to focus on learning and growing in order to be a stronger and wiser person who will fulfill a purpose.

I have created changes to live an amazing life and I certainly still experience things that are not amazing every day. When I don't feel amazing, when my thoughts aren't amazing, or when my reactions to other people aren't amazing, I notice that I'm in a funky space and make a choice to move through it. Sometimes just acknowledging my funk is enough to move through it. I do a flow test and say the words, "This is it and it's perfect...the way it is, and the way it isn't." If I can say this to myself with true inner calm, then I know that I'm in flow. If there's something that I'm still being negative about, I consider what action I need to take to bring myself to let it go and get back in flow.

When I was in a retail store one day, the woman who served me looked dead to the world. The store had a system of signs in the long line of cash registers that allowed a cashier who was free to assist the next customer by pushing a button to light the sign up. The customer would then approach that cashier. But my cashier wasn't pushing her button to welcome the next customer, being me. The cashier beside her, her neighbor, waved me down to go to this cashier. I approached the cash register and the dead-looking cashier stared loathingly at the two wooden nightstands I had piled in the cart to buy. She shuffled slowly and heavily around from the back of the counter to get closer to the cart in order to scan the items. She rang through the transaction, speaking as little as possible. When it came time for me to sign the receipt, she simply placed the paperwork on the counter in front of me without a word.

I began to contemplate finding out this cashier's name so that I could report her to the company for her exceptionally poor attitude and poor customer service, but decided to be curious and compassionate instead. "How's your day going?" I asked. "I have an awful headache. I'm thinking about going home," she replied. "You don't look well," I acknowledged. Her face and body relaxed, as if relieved that someone had acknowledged her existence. "I hope you have a better day," I said as I walked away, having total empathy for what it must be like to feel like living in a dark fog.

In looking at the faces of people as they walk down the street, I'm intrigued to see how light and present or heavy and dead they look. So many people walk around this planet as if it was a burden or obligation to be going about their day. Wherever you are on the spectrum, on a scale from 1 to 10 with 10 being absolutely extraordinary, consider that when you make a choice, you can have it all. Everything in life will start to flow from that. Whether it is health, finances, or something else to overcome, the first step in transformation is committing to it. Too many people accept that an okay life is as good as it gets. There is no universal limit to how many people can lead an exceptional life. But you can't access exceptional if you're not first aware that the present state is not exceptional. You must make a commitment to take action and let it flow until your life becomes absolutely exceptional.

Get Off the Emotional Elephant

"If small things have the power to disturb you, then who you think you are is exactly that: small."

ECKHART TOLLE

We can easily become consumed by our emotions. Rather than us controlling our emotions, they control us. It's like we're on an elephant ride, and the elephant is running absolutely wild. When was the last time you were on one of these emotional elephant rides? An hour ago? Yesterday? Last week? How often does it happen? Do you take mini emotional elephant rides or humungous ones?

Here's the most important question: would you like to take the reins and ride that elephant in a new, slow, and peaceful way?

Emotions are natural, of course. We wouldn't be human without them. Some people say it would be easier to be a goldfish and not have a need to manage emotions, but emotions make us social and connected creatures. We get connection and love out of the deal. In the book of life, these experiences of affinity are not only normal experiences but very desirable ones.

The problem occurs when emotions take over. Physiologically, emotions actually hijack the brain. Many studies in neuroscience are being done every day to better understand when and how this process occurs. It is a fascinating area of learning. Suffice it to say, the higher your emotions get, the less you are able to think rationally. Chemicals are released in your brain, which inhibit your ability to process thoughts in a logical manner.

Emotional elephant rides are inevitable because, as humans, we have emotions. However, we always have the power to choose what kind of ride we're going to go on in any given moment, and how long it's going to last.

Put Yourself ON the Hook

There is certainly an appeal to allowing emotions to take over—it gets us off the hook and makes someone or something besides us responsible. Most of us think that other people, events, and circumstances cause us to feel a certain way. For example, "If my boss wasn't such a jerk, I'd be happy and productive at work." Or "Ugh, it's such a cold, cloudy day that I just feel yucky."

My kids are slowly learning about taking responsibility for their emotions. The other night after I told my daughter it was her brother's turn to do something, she shouted at me, "You are frustrating me!" She didn't want to take turns. I responded, "Honey, I know it may seem like I'm frustrating you, but actually you're choosing to be frustrated. It's your brother's turn. That's it. You can choose to let this go, or you can choose to be frustrated. It's up to you. And whatever you choose, it's still your brother's turn." I nestled up beside her as she pouted and sighed, making it clear that she wanted me to change my mind and say it was her turn. I continued rubbing her back to send the message that I wasn't going to change my mind and that I love her no matter what.

When we fail to manage our emotions, we give up our power. We're continually at the effect of other people and happenings. This is like standing at the top of a mountain and screaming, "I freely give up all power to run my life in the way I see fit. I'm more than happy to be at the effect of whatever happens. I will make excuses for my bad mood and behavior every day. I will blame how I feel and act on anyone or anything else but me."

Now, this is not the beginning of the self-help era. Many of us know that it's not wise or effective to blame others and circumstances for our reactions and where we're at in life. But why do we continue to do it? Why is it so seductive? Why is it so addictive?

Not only do we let ourselves off the hook for being responsible, but we live in a culture in which the media promotes people being on wild, emotional elephant rides. Television shows are full of people living animated, drama-filled lives. And we watch them. For goodness sake, if there was no drama, most people would say the show is boring. Tabloids and magazines are full of stories about family feuds, legal battles, personal secrets, celebrity gossip, etc. It's a vicious circle. The more we watch the shows on television and buy the magazines on the shelves, the more money companies make... and so more of these dramatic television shows and magazines are created for us. If the dramatic material sells and makes money, more dramatic material is created. (For a deeper, and highly interesting look at this notion, read the book *Think: Straight Talk for Women to Stay Smart in a Dumbed-Down World* by Lisa Bloom.)

Identify the Emotional Story

When we are consumed by our emotions, we are immersed in the story and world of those emotions. Think of a recent time when you were caught up in feeling guilty or angry or disappointed or sad or any other emotion. You were likely focusing on and talking about:

- the degree of the emotion;

- the story/events that gave rise to the emotion;

- the actions you were taking to manage the emotion (for example, eating, sleeping, drinking);

- the other events that were happening because of the effect of the emotion on you (for example, getting into a fight with someone else, having difficulty at work, getting physically injured, being short tempered with your kids, having a health condition flare up); and

- how awful the person or circumstance is that caused the emotion.

If I'm feeling angry, I'll want to share with you just how angry I am and what happened to make me this angry. I'll be inclined to elaborate on the story of what happened so that you get the full picture and all the details about why I'm angry. Then I'll tell you about how I'm trying to cope with my anger because it's so overwhelming—for example, I may talk about how I just had to go out for drinks after work to blow off steam, or how I needed to spend the weekend in retreat alone and sleeping, or how the only remedy was some retail therapy. Next I'll want you to know just how much this anger is affecting my life, so I'll talk about the downward spiral that my life is taking because of the anger—maybe I got into a car accident because I couldn't think straight, or I forgot about an important meeting at work because I was so tired from losing sleep. Finally, I'll want you to know how all of this going on is clearly someone or something else's fault. I'll want you to really understand why I'm a victim to somebody else or a circumstance, and how terrible this person or circumstance is.

We become immersed in figuring out, explaining, and justifying our emotional state, which leaves very little, if any, emotional and physical energy to look for the next logical action. This is one of the reasons people hire coaches like me—to support them in seeing past the emotional story to what the real internal block is, and in moving forward in a positive, powerful, and productive way. (Become a member at www.karadcringer.com and receive ongoing resources.)

What world of emotions are you caught up in? Be honest. You may not even want to admit that there's an emotion and story that you've been immersed in. It may even be that you're not aware of how emotional you are because you're almost always emotional about something. This level of emotion and upset is your "normal" life and "just the way it is."

A hint in identifying an emotional elephant ride is to look at the stories you tell other people. If you have repeated the same story or scenario to more than one person, this is likely an emotional elephant ride scenario. If you have many favorite stories that you talk about, you may be on a number of emotional elephant rides.

An emotional elephant ride story often has an element of you being a victim, although it might seem perfectly legitimate for you to complain and be upset about what's happening "to you" in the situation. A story may sound something like, "My neighbors have absolutely no concept of what pride of ownership is. I can't enjoy any of my time at home. I see the apocalypse in their yards as I come home, and look out my windows when I'm trying to enjoy my downtime. Their dogs bark, their kids scream. I can't sleep at night because by the time I go to bed, I have a headache." Or, "My mother has an addiction so she has been erratic and emotionally abusive for years. I can't count on her for anything. I'm the parent to her. My kids suffer because of it. She's an awful role model, and we have no family support."

Reflect on yourself. Look at your emotional world and emotional stories. Write down:

What is an emotional elephant ride that you are on or were on recently?

_____

_____

_____

What stories do you tell yourself and others about the situation?

_____

_____

_____

Who are the people that you blame?

_____

_____

_____

What are the circumstances that you blame?

_____

_____

_____

What aspects of your life are negatively affected by you being on this emotional elephant ride?

_____

_____

_____

Note: Go through these questions for each emotional elephant ride that you are on.

Take the Reins

We have been granted a phenomenal head on our shoulders—a noggin—to help us navigate through life in a calm and empowered manner...but we don't always use it. Have you ever seen two people react to the same thing in a completely different way? Absolutely. It happens all the time. While something may bother one person slightly for a few seconds, the same thing could put another person on an emotional elephant ride for years. When we use our noggin, we take the reins of the emotional elephant ride. We choose to manage our emotions so that we remain in control of our life. Failing to use one's noggin would be like getting on the elephant ride and refusing to use the reins. Why not make full use of the noggin on our shoulders, one of our best life tools, to guide the ride?

One day my son came home from school complaining, "Mom, the kids are calling me skinny!" I said, "Hmm. You are skinny, Honey. You always have been. Even as a baby you were long and skinny. Next time they say, 'You're skinny,' try saying, 'Yes, I am.' That's just the way it is. You may always be skinny. Your friends are trying to see if you'll get upset when they say that, and when you don't get upset, they'll stop saying that to you."

Even at a young age, children can learn that they have full control of their emotions. Just as children are quick to learn languages at a young age, they are also quick to learn life lessons. I believe that life lessons are the greatest gift that we can give children, regardless of their age and our relationship with them. We are all responsible to teach kids this stuff. Certainly we want to be empathetic to their feelings and acknowledge what they are dealing with, but, at the same time, we can coach them to take the reins of their emotions early in life.

A challenge that I give to myself every day is to be an emotionally steady role model for my kids. There are days when I pass with flying colors, and there are days when I fail. With my commitment to being this emotional rock with my kids, every day that I practice I get stronger and stronger in keeping my actions and reactions stable. Months later, a bad day is still far calmer than a good day was. I believe that I have a responsibility to practice what I preach.

One day I was taking my kids to an activity and encouraging them to get dressed and pack their things so that we could make it on time. Sure enough, we arrived at the activity late. As I tried to figure out how we were going to join up with the group that had already left, I found myself becoming short and stern with the kids, essentially telling them to stand still and not say anything while I made a plan. I scolded them and reminded them that I had asked them to hurry when we were getting ready; they hadn't listened and now this was the consequence. My son said, "Sorry, Mom," in a drawn-out, insincere, mundane tone. I wasn't interested in an apology, especially a robotic one. My son's words made me realize that continuing to be angry with them wasn't going to improve the situation or create a learning moment.

I recognized that it was time for me to get in control of the emotional elephant ride, so the three of us got into a huddle. I squatted down to their level so that we could hold eye contact. My commitment is to share with them like partners so that they understand my emotions (that I'm human, too) and so that we learn how to work better together. I shared with the kids that I was disappointed. We had missed the start of the activity and it was now going to be difficult to join in. I explained that when I am urging them to hurry and get ready for something, it's usually because we need to be on time, not just because I'm being grumpy. When we don't get to something on time, we may miss out on the entire activity. Sometimes it's not possible to join in late. I asked what they would do next the time I asked them to get ready quickly. They replied excitedly, "Get ready! Then we can be on time for fun activities!"

When we're on an emotional elephant ride, it's easy to justify that our feelings and reactions are normal and natural given the people and/or circumstances involved. However, a commitment to being emotionally steady requires responsibility for managing emotions in any situation. Many would say I had a right to be angry in that situation. I saw that voicing my anger wasn't going to make a positive difference in that moment or down the road. Yes, it's okay to feel angry, but choosing angry actions and conversation isn't effective.

My commitment to my kids is that we talk about challenges that we encounter and learn together. It's productive to talk about what happened and why and what we are going to do next time. The reflection, learning, and altered action/behavior in the future are what's key in life, for everyone. When we identify our emotions and reflect on what has given rise to them, we can then get logical about what to do the next time in order to create a better outcome. Especially in an interpersonal situation, this understanding is critical in order to learn together about what works and what doesn't. As people, we generally just want to make each other happy and not upset each other, but we need to understand how to create happiness together.

Get Ready!

Okay, here's a pep talk. When an emotion comes up:

- feel it/acknowledge it—defying feelings only makes them stronger

- name it—identifying feelings gives you clues for next actions

- move through it—getting into action is key to flowing through the feelings

Can you think of a time recently when you didn't want to feel the way you did or tried to pretend you weren't feeling the way you did? Many of us resist our own feelings. It's important to take the time and energy to really accept, acknowledge, and work through our own feelings. We often think that feelings are just the way they are and that we need to deal with how they show up in our lives until they evaporate. We expect that, to properly deal with our feelings, we need to hire someone (like a therapist) to help us.

It's common for us to think of our feelings as overwhelming, a nuisance, distracting, or overpowering. Negative feelings, such as anger, resentment, guilt, etc., often lead to yucky sensations in our body. Although we enjoy having positive feelings, such as joy, excitement, etc., it can sometimes seem like even these positive feelings engulf us. Whether negative or positive, feelings can overtake our bodies and minds, hijacking our ability to think clearly and to take rational next steps.

The key is to start taking accountability for your feelings. Feelings are not something that happen to you. Feelings are you. By accepting that feelings come from a deep place within, there is a new space to consider how and why those feelings are emerging and what to do or not do. Rather than being at the effect of our feelings, we can learn from them.

Move Through Feelings

Feelings act as a guidepost for what works and what doesn't work in life. They're like our compass indicating which way we should guide the elephant to go on the ride. When you notice that your feelings are overcoming your ability to think, just notice it. You will get better at noticing when your feelings are overcoming you. This in itself is a step forward. Then let your logic kick in and think about what the feeling is about.

If you feel disappointed, look at what expectations you set up for yourself to be disappointed. Disappointment is all about a fantasy that we create in our minds about how we thought things were going to be. Often we think that others should have done or said something or that circumstances should have been different.

This is based on our own idea of how other people should behave. You may think, "Well, I never would do that." That's true. But the other person did. And that's that. Everyone has their own opinion of what to do or not do in a situation. Everyone's own opinions and behaviors make complete sense to her/him. It's critical to remember that the only thing we have control over is ourselves. When we go with the flow and are accepting of things for how they are and how they aren't, we curb the likelihood that we will be disappointed.

When guilt arises, consider who you're wishing you were. In other words, we all have many notions about who we think we should be—ideally what we would say, how we would behave, what choices we would make. When we feel guilty, it means that we've been a certain way in reality that doesn't match with the way we think we should be in our fantasy. Rather than getting caught up in a negative spiral of getting down on ourselves for not being a certain way, it's far more productive to look at what actions would enhance the current situation and what actions we are committed to for the future.

Jealousy can be one way to look at what it is that you want and don't have, and then to create it. First consider: is this desire based on fantasy or reality? If, for instance, you are jealous of someone's body—toned legs, flat stomach, and strong arms—then maybe it's time for you to get into action and become more lean and strong. But if you're lean and strong and still jealous, then maybe it's time to explore your inner confidence and where that lack of confidence is coming from. Keep checking in with yourself and consider whether your jealousy is based on fantasy or reality. Jealousy can put us into action to create more of what we want in life. If you're jealous of the strength of another couple's relationship, then look at how to create more connection, intimacy, and fun in your relationship. Take action to create more of what you want in life and jealousy will dissipate.

At the same time, remember that our fantastical minds can trick us into thinking that things could always be better than what they are. Another couple may appear to have a rock-solid relationship in public, but we don't always know what goes on behind closed doors. Be grateful for what you have in life. Look at how things are and how things aren't. Practice identifying and embracing the "glass is half full" perspective based exactly on how things are and how things aren't. Set aside wishes, expectations, and stories that life could or should be "better."

If you're feeling angry, think about what personal boundary was pushed. We can contemplate whether to assert our boundaries or whether it is beneficial to simply let go. We need to evaluate whether it's worth the time and energy to push back. When you're angry, first consider if you're angry with yourself for some reason. I know this is counterintuitive because the appeal of being angry is that we get to blame someone else for making us upset. But if we really look deep, the anger can be at ourselves.

When you feel hurt by something someone has said, look at the truth you see in what they've said. When something that someone else says stings, it often means that it has hit a grain of truth within you that you identify with. You need to look within you to know what it is you're questioning, uncertain, or unconfident about in yourself. For instance, if you are 40 years old and someone says in a curt tone, "You're 50 years old," there's a good chance that it won't bother you. The truth is that you're 40. It's a fact. It's as simple as that. There's no emotional reaction. (It would be the same as someone saying the sky is green, when the fact is that the sky is blue.) But if someone says, "You look like you're 50!" you may react because you think they're saying you look old. If you have insecurities about looking old (whatever looking old is in your mind), then comments of this nature will probably bother you. If you have deep confidence in yourself and little concern about looking old, then you'll be far less likely to react. You may even recognize that the person's comment has nothing to do with you.

I used to react when a close family member would inform me that I wasn't being a good mom and give me all of the reasons why s/he thought I was letting the children and her/him down. This person had a tendency to be very direct in her/his comments. I was crippled by the criticism and drowning in the intensity of my emotions. The truth was, which took me a few years to face, I myself was doubting my abilities and success as a mother. I was working full-time, travelling with work, taking on new business commitments, and the kids were young. I was physically and mentally exhausted. I had to take a good look. Facing the true state of my life wasn't easy, and creating a complete transformation in my life in the following years wasn't easy, either. But after I had turned my relationship with myself and my relationship with the kids around, when the close family member tried to criticize me as a mother years later, I could look at her/him straight in the eye with full confidence and assertiveness and say, "That's not true."

When you choose to be hurt and angry, you're letting the other person hurt you and you're losing your energy. If you choose to get over it and move forward, you're taking care of yourself because you're not wasting energy on the situation. (It should be noted that this doesn't necessarily apply to physical or emotional abuse. Further, there are different opinions on where the line is when a situation becomes abusive.)

A powerful relationship to one's feelings can result in creating a newfound level of peace and ease in life. We can practice honoring the feelings and then moving forward. Rather than fighting with ourselves internally, we can learn to recognize the feelings that come up, consider the reasons for the feelings, and keep ourselves on track to living purposefully.

As you may have already recognized, this section could be a book in and of itself. Feelings—and our relationship to them—are a complex phenomenon. For an insightful and thorough exploration of feelings and how to be with them in a powerful way, check out Karla McLaren's book *The Language of Emotions: What Your Feelings Are Trying to Tell You*.

Get Into Action

The amount of time and energy we waste on needless drama and emotion is ridiculous. We get ourselves into a funk, all because we let our emotions take over. We create a story in our minds to legitimize our emotions. If we are feeling sad, we think about what is making us sad, and daydream about all the reasons why the person or circumstance is making us sad. This story justifies our sadness. Then our mind may wander to what else in our life is making us sad. The sadness gets more robust, and hangs around for longer because we are immersed in the story of how and why we are sad.

Often, in order to stop ourselves from running away on a wild, emotional elephant ride, the best thing to do is to be in action and get things done in our lives, in the community, and in the world. When we're focused on being in action in our lives— being productive and continually taking actions aligned with our goals and passion—there's less space to get into the fruitless and annoying spin of our own thoughts.

If I start to get particularly emotional about something, I get into action rather than wallowing in emotion. For instance, I may go to bed. I know that I need about eight hours of sleep, so I may as well go to sleep a little bit earlier and wake up a little bit earlier. I'll most likely wake and be happier and more productive tomorrow. I'll choose to go to bed instead of trying to escape into a television show or unhealthy snack. Now this doesn't mean that I go to bed and sleep for one or two or three extra hours. The whole idea is to take the next action, which is sleeping, in order to get to the next action, which is starting the next day. The intention in taking the next action is to get out of an emotional funk. Taking the next action can be done by making supper, tackling a project, getting some exercise, running an errand. Simply take on the next priority or anything that needs to get done.

We can also look for an action to take in order to move our attention from ourselves to others. Write a card to thank someone, mow a neighbor's lawn, or make a healthy snack to share at work. When we're focused on contributing to others' lives in small and big ways wherever and whenever possible, there's less space to drive ourselves crazy in our own minds. Rather than daydreaming about how something could be or should be in our own lives, we are spending our time and energy on creating love and connection.

It should be noted here that I'm not recommending procrastination. It works to take an action in order to shift emotion, but it doesn't work to continually move to a new action if a particular task overwhelms, bores, or scares you. This is about managing emotions by moving to the next task. This is not about avoiding a task and moving to a new task when emotions arise because you don't want to dig into and complete a particular task. If you notice yourself habitually moving away from a certain task or certain set of tasks, then it's important to identify this as procrastination and deal with the emotions related to why you are avoiding that task or set of tasks.

Chill 66

Often, as I'm writing a particular chapter, something comes up in my own life that perfectly illustrates what I'm writing about. In this situation, I was reminded of how being in action is so effective in getting out of an emotional funk.

I had begun seeing someone new. We had gone on two dates, and with a "you only live once attitude," I chose to be intimate with him on the second date. The sweet and attentive texts that I had consistently been receiving from him subsided after this intimate date. A few days later, on a Friday night, I hadn't received any communication at all from him that day. We had not made plans to see each other that weekend. I received two very short 3 a.m. texts from him Saturday morning. I started to create a story where he thought I was good enough to be intimate with but not good enough to hang out with on the weekend. He seemed, to me, far more interested in being out drinking with his friends than with being with me. I was getting into an emotional spiral, thinking that I had made a mistake in my choice to be intimate with him. We had agreed to date each other exclusively, but I was beginning to think that if he wasn't interested in seeing me on the weekends anyway, I may as well date other people. (Can you hear the emotional story that I was creating?) I was thinking I should set him straight, tell him that I deserve more communication, time, and attention than that, shut my phone off, and ignore any texts from him.

As my emotions were rising and my internal conversation was heightening, I was aware that I didn't want to go any further on this emotional elephant ride, so I got into action. I reached out to a trusted girlfriend. I picked her because I know that she also has a no-drama attitude and that she would set me straight.

After explaining the situation to her, bless her soul, my girlfriend texted me back and said, "It's very early. Y'all have only been on two dates. Maybe wait a bit. People have different pacing with this stuff. Instead of making it a 'here are my expectations conversation,' be curious. Ask him how he sees pacing in general and with you. And share your perspective on this. Remember that thing about not having expectations without agreement. Either your respective pacing will mesh or they won't. It's not more complicated than that. Stay out of story beyond that. Just some thoughts.... Your call, babe."

I sent my girlfriend the following text back: "Yes. Thank you for being so straight. I agree. You're right. Second date and I was the one who made my choice. I expected because he had been so sweet and attentive the week before that it would continue. Those are my own expectations. On his side he may be guessing where I'm at, too. It's the normal easing-into-things phase. I'm always reminded how we as human beings make up stories, exaggerate, etc. Guess I'm still human hey.... This is a good thing. Space and time, and taking it slow is good. I've got a ton of work to do this weekend. And I've got a book to write."

Next, I went to hot yoga and sweated a whole lot of anxiety, guilt, disappointment, self-consciousness, impatience, and confusion out. My mind felt clear, and my body felt empty. After yoga, I went home, showered, and settled down to write. I was focusing my thoughts on being grateful for having a chunk of dedicated time to work and to fulfill my purpose and passion. Four hours later, I received a text from him.

Him: Hi! I was thinking....

Me: ?

Him: I have a trip coming up. ☺

Me: ?

Him: To Mexico. Looking for great company.

Yes, only hours after I had taken the reins of the emotional elephant ride by being in action, he was texting me to invite me on a business trip. I don't think for a second that the timing of this was a coincidence. When I took the reins of my emotions, I believe the energy in the universe shifted to allow for him to bring forward the invitation.

I share this story not because I'm thrilled to share the details of my personal life but because I think it's a very real example of how we create stories and work ourselves into a tizzy when there's absolutely nothing to get worked up about. The emotional elephant ride can take off in a shot, and before we know it, we're allowing negative feelings to consume us. In fact, when we work ourselves up, we often create our own reality by generating negative energy and stories, which then cause the situation to turn sour because of the negative attitude we have developed toward it.

When we get into action and take the reins of the emotional elephant ride, time and energy opens up for positivity to flow. I believe in the law of attraction. I don't think it was a fluke that, in short time after I had calmed myself down and connected to my real priorities in life, I received the text from him.

Pick Your Peeps

It's always wise to be aware of the attitudes and mind frames of the peeps you hang around with and to choose your social circle consciously. Our friends influence how we operate in life, so there certainly is value in considering who we lean on for a listening ear.

An especially good time to be cognizant of who you're chatting with or venting at is when you know:

• you're on an emotional elephant ride;

• you're moving in and out of taking the reins of the emotional elephant ride, and refusing to take the reins of the emotional elephant ride; or

• you've gotten on an emotional elephant ride about situations like this in the past.

Talk to a friend who's not keen on sending you on a wild, emotional elephant ride, or going on a wild, emotional elephant ride with you. Share with a friend who will listen, be empathetic, and be reasonable—not a friend who will fuel your emotions. Some people get a kick out of talking about how awful other people are, how unfair life is, and/or how dramatic situations are. Look to a friend who will help you get logical about the situation— someone who'll challenge your thinking and assumptions, hypothesize about what the other person's intentions may have been, separate the facts from the story you've created, and/or see the gift of learning that will come from the experience.

Reach out to a friend who will hold your hand and go for a slow walk beside you on your elephant ride, rather than give you a boost onto that elephant and send you on a ridiculous ride. You may need to remind your friend that you don't want to go on a ridiculous ride. Encourage your friend to be gracious and to help you to look for the benefit of the doubt in the situation. Ask your friend to help you look deeper into your thoughts and feelings in order to identify why you're emotionally triggered. Ask your friend to support you in letting go of your emotional reaction and figuring out some logical next steps (which may be to not act at all!).

If you're keen on staying on an even keel emotionally, one of the strongest possible supports that you can put in place is to surround yourself with friends who share the same commitment (and who actually live their life that way). For the next while, spend lots of time listening to your friends. Listen to what they talk about and how they talk about it. This will give you insight into what their orientation is regarding emotions and drama. You can then start to choose who you spend time with, and what you talk about with your peeps.

Stop Taking Things Personally

We take way more personally than we need to. Most of the time, people in the world are just living their lives, dealing with their own stuff. In fact, our society these days is so insular that now, more than ever, people are absorbed in what they see as their own individual world. We're all living in our own little bubbles, yet we react to what other people say and do like it has something to do with us.

When people are disrespectful (from your point of view), challenge yourself to be empathetic rather than to react. When someone cuts you off in traffic, or cuts in front of you in line, or cuts you down, it can be a sign that s/he is having a bad moment, bad hour, bad day, bad week, bad month, or bad year. It takes time, practice, and commitment to learn to be empathetic and to not react. It's a new habit. The learning curve may go like this:

1. a negative external and internal reaction—feelings of anger, defensiveness, etc., with body language, words, and/or actions that push back

2. to a negative internal reaction (with no external reaction)—an ability to control your appearance and demeanor, yet still feel frustration, judgement, etc., internally

3. to no reaction (internal or external)

You know you have developed empathy and a habit of no reaction when you can smile kindly and authentically wish someone the best regardless of what they say and do. No matter what someone else's words or actions are, they roll off you like water off a duck's back.

One powerful tool in not taking things personally is to look at what the person said or did versus what you interpreted it to mean. Often we amplify or exaggerate comments or behaviors, assuming that people had negative intentions behind what they said or did. In the beginning, as you learn to use this tool, first challenge yourself to replay the situation. If a video recorder or sound recorder captured the moment, what are the true facts (without interpretation) of what happened? Then do a double check. Ask yourself: if a complete stranger assessed the situation, what would s/he report on the facts of what happened? Which parts of how you are assessing or interpreting the situation are actually fact and which parts are stories that you've created?

Next, take time to really reflect on the stories that you've created about the situation. Identify what actually happened (the action), and then ask yourself, "What did I make that mean?" For instance, if your significant other arrives home late on a special occasion and says that work was especially busy that day, you may make this mean that you are not important, or s/he doesn't care about you, or s/he is ignorant and selfish, or something else. This is story. The action is arriving home late. The story is your interpretation of what arriving home late means. This meaning making and story is what sets off the emotional elephant ride.

Perhaps the truth is that work was especially busy that day and your partner arrived home late because there was work to complete. Arriving home late has nothing to do with you. Arriving home late has everything to do with work being busy that day. That's it. That's the fact.

I've learned that when people are curt, sarcastic, rude, hostile, or whatever flavor of "disrespect" they're showing, it says more about them than me. Recently, when someone said something cutting to me, my mouth nearly dropped open in shock and I caught myself thinking, "Holy cow! I can't believe that I just heard you say that! I don't think I would ever say that." One of the gifts a close family member gave me was to learn how to act with highly abrasive comments. It took me many years to really understand and accept that the comments had absolutely nothing to do with me. Her/his attitude and words reflected the way s/he had learned to communicate and the deep unhappiness that was within.

This is not to say that we can let ourselves off the hook of taking responsibility when others are upset and simply say that any upset is all about other people overreacting. It's always key to look at how we've contributed to any situation and to take full ownership. By being overly generous in taking ownership of anything and everything that we contributed, we create a clear and open space for the situation to shift and a higher probability (not a guarantee) that the other person will also look at her/his contribution.

At a deeper level, we are all connected in the world. By saying, "Don't take things personally," I don't mean to say that you should create more distance between you and the next person. It's actually the opposite. If we see the inherent connection among all of us as beings, we can extend kindness to others, especially in the times when they're most needed—when they're being distant, accusatory, angry, or whatever else. The result of this is an untouchable state of calm and acceptance that resounds within you. Rather than wasting energy on focusing on emotions and experiences that are negative, we can be focusing on what we're grateful for and what we're creating and contributing in the world.

Hold Your Power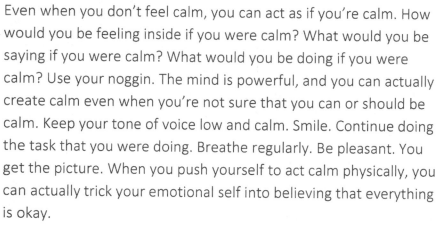

Even when you don't feel calm, you can act as if you're calm. How would you be feeling inside if you were calm? What would you be saying if you were calm? What would you be doing if you were calm? Use your noggin. The mind is powerful, and you can actually create calm even when you're not sure that you can or should be calm. Keep your tone of voice low and calm. Smile. Continue doing the task that you were doing. Breathe regularly. Be pleasant. You get the picture. When you push yourself to act calm physically, you can actually trick your emotional self into believing that everything is okay.

When we allow emotions to skyrocket, we can become paralyzed for hours, days, weeks, or even years. By putting one foot in front of the other in life—even just in keeping on in daily activities—we minimize the time and space we have to continue creating stories in our minds, escalating the feelings and the drama. When we care for ourselves in a positive way—by doing activities such as exercising, eating a healthy meal, going for a massage, having a short nap, getting outside into fresh air and sunshine, drinking water, etc.—we also minimize the chance of digging ourselves further into a rut. By chatting with a friend who will talk us down (not up), we further reduce the chances of getting on an emotional elephant ride. At one time, my coach,

Matt Thorpe, would say, "If you're in your head for more than an hour girl, call me."

Think of a situation and answer the following questions:

What have you been emotional about?

_____

_____

_____

_____

What are the exact emotions that you've been feeling?

_____

_____

_____

_____

How are your emotions paralyzing you?

_____

_____

_____

_____

What next action(s) would be beneficial to take?

_____

_____

_____

_____

Mastering the ability to get off the emotional elephant ride, and the tendency to not let it get away in the first place, is a skill and an art that requires ongoing commitment and practice. This is not about becoming a monk. It's about shifting the way we choose to live life—choosing not to let people and circumstances take hold of us; choosing to learn about ourselves in order to enhance our self-understanding and interpersonal relationships; choosing to live in reality rather than story; choosing to care for our emotional and physical health; and choosing to be with people who are committed to all of the same.

There are many exceptional personal and professional development programs in the world. The most powerful courses that have supported me in moving through emotional blocks, and in training to live free from emotional elephant rides, has been the ones I have taken with Landmark Worldwide. They offer programs in many, many cities and countries around the world. Their first course is called The Landmark Forum. It is extremely affordable for a course of this caliber and it offers unbelievable value, especially if you go into the course open minded and keen to be honest with yourself. I highly recommend The Landmark Forum and Landmark Worldwide's other courses.

Honor Your Body as a Temple

"Number one, like yourself. Number two, you have to eat healthy. And number three, you've got to squeeze your buns. That's my formula."

RICHARD SIMMONS

We need a wake-up call when it comes to health, and there are many stats that reveal this. In Canada, one in four adults and one in 10 children have clinical obesity. Recent studies indicate that less than five percent of American adults get the recommended 30 minutes of physical activity per day. What is everyone doing if they aren't exercising? Usually watching television. Americans and Canadians are said to watch four to five hours of television per day. People are also eating more and more fast food. Between 2004 and 2014, consumer spending on fast food increased by over 30 percent in the U.S.

A healthy body is life. Literally. Period. Simple. That's it. Without health, we have nothing. The pleasures of life cannot be enjoyed if we're ill and certainly not if we're dead. Nobody wants to deal with pain, constipation, dizziness, nausea, or any other symptom. These symptoms drag us down as we go about our day, sometimes keep us at home, or even put us in the hospital.

Make a Choice

If there's going to be a change to the status quo and what has been acceptable for your health over the last number of weeks, months, or years, there needs to a marked point where a choice is made. It's not saying, "Yeah, I could probably do better," or "I should probably start taking better care of my health." The marked point is where you choose that health is a priority for you. There are always going to be many other necessary, fun, and relaxing priorities competing with health like working, shopping, drinking, cleaning, Facebooking, etc., but remember: nothing in the world will generate happiness if you have poor health. We need to choose health first.

Don't expect that one day you will have an epitome, choose that health is your number one priority, and feel your whole life change immediately. The transformation to put health first is a process that requires us to make commitments, take action, and build new habits. My journey in learning about health and nutrition and making shifts in my lifestyle has unfolded over time—and will continue to unfold—with some marked wake-up calls along the way.

One wake-up call for me happened a few years ago when I realized that I spent more time and money driving and maintaining my Volkswagen Touareg than exercising and caring for my body. I'd spend hours waiting in the shop for an oil change and pay for premium oil. I would fill it up with premium gas. I would pay for it to be waxed. I would clean the interior. When I recognized that I wasn't spending the same amount of time, money, and energy on my body, I decided that I needed a significant shift in my lifestyle. Rather than putting premium gas in my vehicle, I needed to start putting premium food in my real vehicle—my body. It was high time to start spending my precious hours on nurturing the foundational vehicle of my life.

Another wake-up call occurred at an annual conference that I attended. In one of the sessions, we were setting personal and professional goals. I remember turning to the gal next to me and saying, "I want a body like yours." She was very lean. She looked at me with surprise and said in a concerned tone, "No, you don't. I'm not healthy. I don't eat. I run around all day and don't even take care of myself." Wow. That was not what I was expecting to hear. It was definitely food for thought, so to speak. I sat in my chair thinking. After a few minutes, I wrote on my goal sheet that I was committed to being "lean and mean" by next year's conference. Then I reminded myself of the importance of using clear and powerful words when goal setting. I crossed out "lean and mean" and wrote "lean and clean." In writing down my goal, I could feel a new level of commitment and clarity behind it.

Yet another wake-up call was when I was shopping for swimsuits before an upcoming trip to Florida. Post two children, I found myself at the store picking out one-piece suits and tankinis. I took half a dozen of my suit picks over to my mom's house to try them on. She has always been my bathing suit critique extraordinaire; I know she is going to be honest. She asked why I didn't have any two-piece suits, and I said that I wasn't going to wear a two-piece with a mommy tummy. Bless her heart, my mom assured me that this was completely normal—after kids this is the reality, and I may never feel sexy wearing a two-piece again. I contemplated how quick we can be to jump to apathy and acceptance and use circumstances as an excuse for something undesirable in life.

Measure, Measure

One of the keys to starting a new chapter in your health is to seek out some statistics on you. Find out what your starting point is and get a baseline. Log the food that you eat in a day. Buy a pedometer or Fitbit to get a base count of your daily activity. Have a body composition completed. Test your heart rate and blood pressure. Get your measurements done. Many gyms offer consultations for free or at a nominal charge. If you are at a gym or looking into a gym that doesn't offer consultations for free or at an affordable rate, consider looking for a different gym.

This objective information is essential to measure progress and identify accomplishments. Measurements of the status quo create a baseline for calculating progress. One of the successes of the Weight Watchers program is that everything is measured and tracked. Numbers are factual. They tell the true story of any steps forward or backward in performance.

There's power in looking at pure fact, without the story. Looking at measurements of the status quo gets you out of fantasy and into reality. The stories and reasons why your health is not where it could be are irrelevant. Our bodies will change over time, sometimes depending on our circumstances. However, it's critical that we maintain our health and fitness level regardless of the excuses in our life not to.

Because there are so many aspects to health, it's important to evaluate our progress from a number of different standpoints. The indication of health and fitness is not displayed on the scale by the number of pounds, but by measures such as muscle mass, BMI, blood pressure, etc. Even one single measure of calorie or fat intake is not an indication of the quality of one's diet.

It seems that most people are motivated to measure their performance in other areas of life, especially when a certain level of performance is required, yet in the area of health, it's not usually of interest or a high priority. We pay attention to entrance exam scores, workplace performance reviews, the number of Facebook friends we have, safety ratings, budget reports, YouTube video views, and sports league stats. We're certainly keen to monitor the academic performance of our children. But when it comes to our bodies, it seems that we aren't at all thrilled to seek the numbers and know the hard facts about where we stand with our health.

Why is it that people avoid performance checks in the area of health? In general, we're a society that's apathetic and lazy when it comes to health and fitness. Whether you're skinny or fat, eat too little or too much, there's a strong element of avoiding the real work that it takes to turn things around and live a healthy lifestyle.

The bar is set low in terms of what average health is so we can easily justify that bad-to-average health is acceptable. This gets us off the hook of really looking at the level of our health and taking diligent action to ensure our health. As long as we walk down the street and don't stick out like a sore thumb—as long as we are mobile and look within the range of "normal"—we can assure ourselves that our health is okay.

It doesn't work to measure your own health relative to the health of others, especially since the bar is so low. We justify our own bad habits by pointing to the bad habits of others. We may say something like, "Well, it's okay that I eat too much chocolate because I don't smoke or drink." Or "I do drink 10 cups of coffee each day, but I don't eat fast food." When you compare your health against bad health, you're going to stay stuck in bad health.

It's time to stop pretending that being unhealthy is okay because so many other people are unhealthy. Being healthy is not just for certain people—famous people, people who have time, people who are born that way. Being healthy is essential for every single person's body, mind, and soul. It's a day-to-day and ongoing commitment to eat a healthful diet and get exercise in order to live long, strong, and in song.

It's also time to stop measuring our health against media images. Healthy isn't likely the size two model in the magazine. We are a society that has taught people—largely through media—that skinny is beautiful and to be skinny you need to eat less.

We often don't even realize how ingrained these thoughts are in us. Years ago, I remember a family member saying that she didn't like the look of her friends who were avidly working out. She said they didn't get skinnier, their fat just turned to muscle. She didn't think they looked better at all. Many of us have been programmed to think that we need to strive to be skinnier. At the gym about a year ago, I was upset that my weight had actually increased slightly over six months despite my ongoing commitment to regular workouts and a clean diet. A trainer gently reminded me that muscle weighs more than fat. She pointed out that the measurements of my thighs and arms had decreased.

Certainly eating in moderation is an element of a healthful diet, but we must get over the notion that beautiful is skinny. "Strong is the new skinny" is one of my favorite slogans. I encourage myself to admire different body shapes of healthy women, with some being tall and slim, and others being shorter and curvier. What I focus on is the glow in other women's cheeks, their energy, and their confidence.

It may be time to look at revamping our notions of what health is and who it's for. Health is for everyone, but it doesn't have to look like a size two or a size zero. Let's put good food and movement in our days, strive to make and measure our own goals, focus on what feels good for our bodies and minds, and worry less about comparing ourselves to the people in the magazines and on television.

Say What's On the Line

Think about what you would get out of being healthy and fit. What's on the line for you? What's the carrot for you? It's probably a number of things. Maybe it's feeling sexy; fitting into your existing wardrobe; having the energy to volunteer; playing freely with your kids; enjoying an enhanced sex life; being able to do your job easier; getting a good night's sleep; or living longer. The list goes on and on.

There is a lot on the line for me in maintaining my health. Right now, if I had to pick both my kids up, one in each arm, and sprint for safety, I know that I could because I'm fit and strong. I wanted this extra level of confidence as a parent. I also wanted to be a role model. It's important to me to send a message that health is a priority and that the other priorities of work, family, and fun can still be tended to. And I wanted to feel sexy with my partner and enjoy an intimate sexual relationship.

Without even knowing it or thinking of it, there may be a number of things that you are missing out on or avoiding because of a lack of health. For example, maybe even unconsciously, you avoid going on a warm vacation with your partner or a friend because you don't want to wear a swimsuit. Maybe you're grumpy on a day-to-day basis because you're dehydrated, over-caffeinated, and/or fat. Maybe you're sick. Maybe you don't like going to events or being in public places because you worry that people are judging you. You're tired. You're self-conscious. You're cranky. You're anti-social. You're lazy. Push yourself to look for consequences of lack of health in your life. Look for consequences that you may not have even known were there. Be honest with yourself. What are you forfeiting for bad health, and what would you gain from good health?

What are you forfeiting by being unhealthy?

_____

_____

_____

_____

_____

What would you gain from being healthy?

_____

_____

_____

_____

_____

It's a selfish act to not take care of your body. Depending on the level of ill health, there's an impact on those around you. They may not be able to spend as much time with you and have fun. They may see you down or depressed and worry. They may see you upset with them and be offended or hurt. They can become seriously concerned for you, affecting their own energy and health. They may actually need to care for you. At a wider reach, you may be drawing on insurance or health programs that others are paying into. (As the average health of people in society goes down, payment rates into such plans and programs go up.)

I want to make it clear that I'm not saying that anyone deserves to be sick and that it has happened because s/he has been selfish and not cared for her/his health. What I'm saying is that we all have a responsibility to learn about health and to care for our bodies. We have a responsibility to take action to enhance our health so that we're healthy and happy, connected to the people around us, and able to contribute to our communities, rather than relying on programs and services to care for us. (Check out Louise Hay's book *You Can Heal Your Life* for wonderful teachings on taking self-responsibility for your own health. As Hay says, "When we are willing to do the mental work, we can heal anything.")

Dig Into Your Diet

Diet is a fundamental pillar to health and fitness. If you're not eating good food, you may not have the energy to exercise, and your food choices will counteract your exercise. Diet is a complex matter and there are books upon books that can guide you with advice on diet. There seem to be as many different philosophies on diet as there are pairs of shoes or kinds of men in the world. Diet is not simple. What is critical is that you make a commitment that diet will be a focus for transformation.

We can retrain ourselves when it comes to diet. Some kids in the world learn to eat rice and vegetables, others seaweed, others curry, and others fish sticks. We have been trained throughout our lives to eat and like certain things. When you reflect on what you eat and don't eat, consider how your diet got to be this way. Perhaps it was what you learned or didn't learn growing up, or from the norms in your line of work, or the things you have read along the way, which may be true or untrue. Think about or observe what your parents or guardians eat or ate. Do they, or did they, have a tendency to go for carby foods, fatty foods, sugary foods, processed foods, fast foods? This isn't about making our parents or guardians wrong. It's about gaining awareness about how our diet has been influenced over time and how we got to be where we are at.

The process of learning about health began for me in University when my best girlfriend was working toward a degree in physical education and recreation and taking some nutrition classes. I began to learn what was healthy and unhealthy. I slowly became aware that I had grown up not having any awareness that chicken fingers, perogies, and muffins were not healthy choices. I drank milk and juice and soda throughout the day. Not water.

We can reteach ourselves and teach our kids how to eat and drink. With my kids, we have created a game around talking about what is healthy, what is tasty, and what is healthy and tasty. Apples are healthy, apple pie is tasty, and homemade apple sauce (with no sugar) is healthy and tasty.

My kids know what the expectations are around food. They know that they need to eat fruits and vegetables at every meal. It's one way that I help them to keep stability in their moods. At the resort we were staying at in Mexico, they would attend a kids program in the morning for a few hours while I worked and exercised. One day, I met up with them after lunch. I asked them what they had eaten for lunch and there was no mention of any fruits or vegetables. Going forward, I would pick them up from the kids program just before lunch so we could eat together. This is because a healthy diet is so integral and fundamental to their well-being.

Diet is not simple. It can be hard just to know what food to buy. Eating healthy doesn't mean eating less carbs, sugar, fat, or any other one element. If the product is fat free, it's often chalk full of sugar. Due to commercialism, when we look on the shelves at the grocery store, there are many different kinds of yogurt, peanut butter, cereal—you name it. Thirty years ago people didn't have this kind of choice at the supermarket. How do we know what to pick?

Once we figure out what seems to be the healthy choice among the selection of foods, changing circumstances or new research may point us to a different food choice. For example, if there has been environmental contamination in a body of water, given the circumstances, it's likely wise to avoid eating fish from those waters. Or, if a research study has unveiled health concerns about a certain ingredient, it's likely wise to avoid foods containing that ingredient.

Diet is both simple and not simple because what is simple is to eat more whole, natural foods. If there is a choice between name-brand peanut butter and fresh peanut butter made direct from the peanuts in front of you (we used to have one of these machines years ago in my parents' bulk food store), the healthier choice is obvious. It may not be the tasty choice in your mind, but it certainly is the healthier one.

When the kids and I play our healthy and tasty game, I ask them, "What's healthy...carrots or French fries?" If they answer,

"French fries," I say, "No, French fries are tasty, but they're not healthy." Over the years, we've gotten more sophisticated in our games with questions like, "What's healthy...a smoothie or a banana?" We can then talk about how the answer to the question depends on the smoothie. Often the smoothies at a fast food restaurant aren't made with real fruit and contain high amounts of sugar. The smoothies we make at home are made with real fruit and contain less sugar. We know exactly what we're eating because we've prepared the food and used whole, natural foods.

Another simple choice related to diet is picking raw foods. Raw fruits and vegetables contain the most nutrients and require the least amount of preparation. As snacks and before most meals, I put out a plate of fruits and vegetables for my kids. One likes apples and the other likes grapes, so I put out both. One likes cucumbers and the other likes peppers, so I put out both. They're hungry before the meal so they load up on healthy foods before the meats and carbs are ready for feasting. There are a kajillion different ideas on Pinterest about foods to prepare. I don't know about you, but I rarely have time to delve into them. What I do have time for is washing an apple and a pepper, and cutting them into pieces.

When buying packaged foods, it's extremely beneficial to be adept at reading the nutritional labels. When considering two, three, or more products, use the nutritional labels to make healthier diet choices. Get educated on how to read these labels. Again, it's not just one thing you're looking for. Just because they are gluten free doesn't mean the cookies are healthy.

I strongly believe that just as the composition of our personality is unique, so is the composition of our body and our dietary needs. It's important to find a diet that fits. Consider seeing a naturopath to explore which foods work well for your body and which don't. For me, carbs are a big no-no. More than anything, I love a big plate of pasta, or a sandwich made of fresh gooey white bread, or pizza. Over time I realized that I was getting bloated and gassy when I ate carbs. Because I ate so many carbs, this was the way I felt. I didn't know any different and didn't know that anything was out of whack. It was like a blind spot that I couldn't see. When I cut down on my carbs, I noticed a dramatic difference in how I felt. When I reduced my carbs further, I felt even better. And when I increased my carb intake, I noticed that I felt bloated and gassy about 15–20 minutes after eating the carbs.

It's difficult to know what to cut out of a diet and what the effect will be until you do. Try going on an elimination diet, just for fun. Yes, I did say "just for fun." For me, the fun of going on an elimination diet was increasing awareness around how my body reacted to different types of foods when I reintroduced them and being reminded that my mind is extremely powerful. I saw how I'm fully capable of mind over matter—that even though I didn't really want to, I eliminated sugar, soy, dairy, peanuts, gluten, eggs, and corn. Pick your flavor of elimination and take it on as if your life depends on it. (In fact, your life may actually depend on it.) Don't allow yourself to quit part way through. Better yet, make a Plan B that if you do quit the elimination diet, you will go on the diet again. I'm guessing that this will be enough motivation to complete the diet the first time.

Dietary needs may change from day to day and over time. It's important to accept that just as our journey in relationships evolves, so does our journey in health. We can learn to listen to what our body needs. This intuition takes practice. It can be as simple as asking yourself silently which choice would be more beneficial—chicken or beef or vegetables for instance. After being a near vegetarian for years, when I was pregnant with my first, all of a sudden I started craving and eating beef of all kinds—roast beef, prime rib, steak, hamburgers, etc.

Diet and food can be a love-hate relationship. Many people look forward to going on a cruise or to an all-inclusive resort where they have a feast laid out in front of them for every meal of every day. Recently, someone shared with me that she likes the bacon and the croissants at her favorite all-inclusive, and because of that, she comes home with some extra pounds on her body. Another way to look at holidays is the best time to cut some crappy habits. Whether you're ordering in a restaurant or picking at a buffet, you can make a choice. Plus, there's (hopefully) far less stress and way more time than what you'd have on an average day at home. You can choose fruits and vegetables.

Having a healthy diet isn't about giving up all of the luxuries in my opinion. That would not be chill. That would be extreme. But there does need to be some sacrifice. I love lattes. If I'm choosing, these days I'll go for a Starbucks latte (half sugar) instead of a piece of chocolate cake. I love ice cream, so I go for the yogurt or sorbet (keeping in mind that even though the fat is lower, the sugar is higher). I also love pizza. When I was in New York years ago, I ate pizza all day every day. We often make pizza at home, allowing us to put more veggies and more sauce on. I find the more sauce there is, the less cheese I need. I'm a big fan of hamburgers. I love a good, juicy, beefy hamburger. When I have a hamburger, I take the grease in the meat and the carbs in the bun. But I skip out on the mayo (or any other creamy sauce they want to put on), bacon, and cheese. And I spend extra money on my hamburger at a place where they use good-quality beef.

Find your own strategies, and as you take small steps toward eating cleaner, your body will thank you and ask for more. It can be a peaceful and happy shift. If you like chicken fingers, try breading small pieces of chicken breast at home and baking them. Other choices, like drinking Coke, you may need to just stop. Yes, there is Coke Zero and Diet Coke, but they contain aspartame (not to mention that you could still probably be addicted to the taste of Coke). Start exploring alternatives that help you to gradually shift your diet and taste preferences. For instance, instead of white refined sugar, go for raw sugar, honey (better yet, raw unpasteurized honey), or Stevia. After years of having a hamburger addiction, many times my body now asks for a veggie burger when I'm ordering my meal and happily thanks me after I eat the veggie burger. Diet can and will shift over time, especially on a path of committing to eat cleaner and listening to our bodies.

For the last 15+ years, and especially in the last two years, I've been engaged in a continual process of learning about diet and nutrition. Now it's completely normal for me to take a small container of chia seeds with me to a breakfast buffet so that I can add them to my fruit and yogurt. Sprouted bread now tastes just as good as white bread. I can no longer taste the protein powder that I put in my smoothies. I'm now happy to eat organic black bean spaghetti noodles instead of whole wheat noodles. (The first step was replacing my white spaghetti noodles with whole wheat noodles.) When I buy a takeout stir-fry, I bring it home to mix with spinach and make two or three meals out of it. The choices that I make now and consider normal for me are choices I wasn't even aware of, or certainly never would have dreamed I would do, years ago.

Look at the Whole Picture

Obviously we all know that health is the whole package: diet, exercise, rest, etc. There are many, many elements to health. We're not going to discuss all of the elements here or get into any element in great depth. This is not a book about increasing knowledge. If that's what you're into, there are millions of books around the world that advise on general health and particular aspects of health. Knock yourself out and start learning. I promise it will be well worth the time.

Just as diet is a fundamental building block, so is exercise. Exercise must become a priority. Period. Get your heart rate up for at least 20 minutes per day. That may look like going for a walk on your break at work instead of consuming sugary coffee, staff room pastries, and/or something from the vending machine. There's a good chance you'll want a glass of water after the walk instead of your usual indulgences. Do a game of tag with your kids, or throw them around in the swimming pool. Have some active sex in the morning or evening. Your partner will most likely enjoy this idea.

Another key element of health is rest. I'm not a doctor or a sleep expert. What I will say is that it's common knowledge that adequate rest is critical. Like diet, I believe that each person needs different amounts of rest. I believe that it's important to distinguish the vital necessity of rest from the tendency to use rest as a coping mechanism when we feel disempowered in life. It's a matter of finding a sleep schedule that works for our unique bodies and lifestyle and ensuring that we provide our bodies with the necessary rest to refuel.

A friend of mine used to get seven to eight hours of sleep per night and wake up exhausted. After completing a number of personal development programs, he discovered that he now needs fewer hours of sleep at night to feel rested because he's empowered in his life and on track with his goals and plans. As he created empowerment in his life, he found that he would naturally wake up after about six hours of sleep and have the energy to go all day. Now when he's still tired after getting six hours of sleep, the first question he asks himself is if he is empowered in his life.

There's a ton of value in mastering the skill of taking quick, 20-minute power naps. I've learned this skill myself over the years and have trained myself to sleep anywhere at any time. I once heard on a radio show about a man who had trained his body to work around the clock. He would work for a few hours, take a 20-minute nap, and then work for another few hours throughout the day and night. He has lived like this for years. I'm not an advocate of this lifestyle. What the story does say is that our bodies are very trainable. There's something to be said for being a master at rejuvenating in a 20-minute window. Throw your car in park (safely), tilt back the seat, and catch a few zzzs. On the 40-minute bus or train ride, set an alarm for 20 minutes and close your eyes. In the stands at your kids' activity, go ahead and drift off. (Admittedly, I've done this.) Are you someone who's saying, "I can't do that!"? Well, you're probably right. Maybe you can't right now, but you can learn. When you were six months old, you probably couldn't walk. But you learned. Just do it.

In each aspect of your health, you're responsible for determining what's going to work for you. For instance, to have more fresh fruits and vegetables in the home, it may work for you to have an organic basket delivered to your doorstep. It may work for you to visit a local famer's market. It may work for you to plant a garden.

As we are each a unique human being, the answers to creating our own healthful lifestyle are unique and multifaceted. Creating health in the mind and body requires more action steps than to simply stop drinking soda and take the stairs. The starting point is to recognize, and own, that you're in charge. Someone can tell you what to do or not to do for a healthful lifestyle, but it's important to look at the whole picture in your own life and make choices you are committed to.

Start Somewhere

So, given that a lot of this information isn't new to you, what are you going to do with it? I'm pretty sure you know to drink water, eat fruits and vegetables, and get adequate rest. That's right...knowing makes no difference. You know you should consume less sugar. You know you should exercise instead of watching television. You know you should avoid processed and fast foods. Knowing. Makes. No. Difference.

Given that more knowledge about health isn't what makes the difference, starting somewhere is about making a choice and getting into action. It actually doesn't matter where you start. Do something. Pick something to give up (like smoking, drugs, sugar, coffee, processed foods, alcohol), or pick something to take on (like eating more whole, organic vegetables and foods). Wherever you are at in your health is fine. It is what it is. Like anything else in your life, you can take on transforming your health bit by bit. So given where you're at now, start somewhere—as you either begin your health journey or start your health journey anew.

In pondering my mom's comment about accepting the possibility of never feeling sexy in a two-piece swimsuit again, I was reminded of a promise I made to myself prior to becoming a mom. I had committed that I would always be a "yummy mommy." In other words, I was committed that the demands of being a mom wouldn't interfere with my very most basic needs of staying healthy and fit. So if I'm going to refuse to accept that I will never feel sexy in a two piece again, "What's the next step?" I asked myself.

I contemplated my next action step to deal with my mommy tummy and considered what an ideal plan of action would be. What would I do if I had unlimited resources? Obviously celebrities are able to restore their figures. I mean, we're surrounded by their pictures pre-pregnancy, at pregnancy, and post-pregnancy. A personal trainer could surely kick my butt. Hiring a personal chef would be lovely. A nutritionist would educate me.

The key in choosing to do something different and go after a goal is to start somewhere. When it comes to enhancing health, there's endless information to help you become knowledgeable and there are endless possibilities of steps to take. It's easy to get overwhelmed and not know where to start. We can become so fixed on the right first step or the right plan of action that we don't do anything. To start somewhere in creating a "yummy mommy" figure, I headed to the gym to ask about personal training.

Pick one new habit that you're willing to take on in order to start somewhere. It may seem small, but we're talking baby steps here. Small steps are going to make the difference. One of my girlfriends, Coach Laurie, started doing a 25-minute workout video every morning. (You'll read more about her story in the last chapter of this book.) She had no idea that this would transform her life.

What's one habit you are willing to tackle in the next week? To get you thinking, here are some ideas of possible habits to take on. Come up with an idea that you are committed to.

- Drink eight glasses of water per day.

- Pack fruits and vegetables for snacks.

- Eat less and at better times.

- Attend an exercise class three times per week.

- Stop drinking soda and juice.

- Eat more whole foods.

- Take a walk on break at work.

- Record all food and drinks.

- Walk instead of drive.

- Learn how to read nutrition labels.

- Buy more organic foods.

A habit I'm committed to is:

_____

Now that you've chosen your habit, what are 10 mini tasks you can implement to make this happen? Think about what would make this easier for you, details you need to take care of, what you need to prepare, things that may get in your way, etc.

My 10 mini tasks are:

1. _____

2. _____

3. _____

4. _____

5. _____

6. _____

7. _____

8. _____

9. _____

10. _____

For example, if you chose "drink eight glasses of water," maybe 10 mini tasks look like:

1. Drink a glass of water first thing in the morning and before going to bed.

2. Get a jug that filters water.

3. Stock up on lemons, strawberries, and cucumbers to add to my water.

4. Keep a water bottle in the car.

5. Have a glass of water before each of my meals.

6. Eat spicy food.

7. Download an app on my phone to keep track of my glasses.

8. Have a discussion about the benefits of drinking water and commit as a family that we will drink water at meal times.

9. Have ice in the freezer (if you like your water cold).

10. Commit to myself to only order water when I am eating out.

If you chose "attend an exercise class three times per week," 10 mini tasks could be:

1. Ask Rebecca if she wants to do an exercise class instead of coffee.

2. Plan a routine that has variety in type and intensity of exercise.

3. Register for a class.

4. Review the class schedule and pick days and times that work.

5. Tell five people about my commitment to do three classes per week.

6. Put the classes in my calendar.

7. Arrange child care.

8. Pack gym bag.

9. Put new gym shorts on birthday wish list.

10. Find a friend to check in with and kick my butt.

If you chose "eat more whole foods," 10 mini tasks could be:

1. Go to the farmer's market.

2. Add raw honey to my coffee instead of sugar.

3. Buy only whole foods at the grocery store.

4. Clean out the pantry and donate packaged foods.

5. Cook one or two large meals to create leftovers.

6. Buy coconut oil.

7. Clean and chop fresh vegetables.

8. Learn about the benefits of eating raw food.

9. Substitute white carbohydrates for whole wheat.

10. Replace unhealthy snacks with healthy ones in the house.

If you chose "learn how to read nutritional labels," 10 mini tasks could be:

1. Do a Google search on how to read nutritional labels.

2. Talk with my partner about wanting to learn about nutritional labels.

3. Learn about carbohydrates.

4. Learn about protein.

5. Learn about sugar.

6. Make an appointment with a nutritionist.

7. Watch a YouTube video.

8. Talk to Jessica who is knowledgeable.

9. Borrow a book from the library.

10. Buy healthier granola bars this week by reading the nutritional labels.

The more personal you can get with your strategies, the better. You know what's going to work for you. Sure, everyone could benefit from drinking a glass of water first thing in the morning. Is that something that will work for you? Maybe rather than downloading a water tracker app on your phone, you create a buddy that you check in with at the end of each day to share with each other how many glasses of water you drank throughout the day. Maybe you create a chart to put on your fridge and track your water consumption as a game.

Forming new habits is the key to transforming health. And you can decide if you're more of a cold-turkey or ease-into-it kind of person. My preference has been slow and steady. Nothing crazy ridiculous. That said, maybe diving straight in works for you. Forming a habit can take different people different lengths of time, depending on what new habit they're taking on.

I challenge you to transform your health one habit at a time by starting somewhere with each one. Once the habits and lifestyle have been developed, the hardest work is done. You're out of the vicious circle of lack of energy and feeling lazy, eating out of apathy, boredom, and guilt, and all of the other things that go along with being caught up in an unhealthful day-to-day routine. Cheers to Day One of you starting somewhere and beginning to form new habits!

Create Support

Why do this alone? More and more, I recognize that when I'm not successful in getting something done (whether I think I know how to do it or not), I simply need to reach out and ask for help. We're a community of people in this world for a reason. The most successful people in life create a network of support around them, eat humble pie, and take advice and direction from experts. Just as you often need to hire experts to care for your vehicle, it's wise to hire experts to support you in caring for your body. I obviously hadn't been successful at creating a "yummy mommy" figure post-children, so it was time for a different plan of action.

If resources (time, money, etc.) seem like they're an obstacle for you when looking at setting out strategies or getting professional help, then get creative about it. When I made the choice to create a bikini body, I hired a personal trainer. And here's where the financial creativity comes in. I hired a personal trainer who leads group training sessions so that the cost was substantially lower. The best part was that it turned out our training group consisted of two people. I got the one-on-one attention that I needed at a price that was appealing. It was approximately one-quarter of the cost and nearly all the service. Pure awesome.

Here's another idea: start talking to people about healthy eating and living. Start sharing healthy ideas such as putting chia seeds in water or visiting a new organic market, rather than gossiping about others, criticizing government spending, talking about Sara's new haircut, or bragging about the new watch you bought. When you have a choice, ask the health nut out for a coffee or walk date, rather than your regular drama queen friend. When you create an environment around you that supports healthy living, there's no getting out of it.

Celebrate Breakthroughs

I've been working on my health, building new habits, and shifting my lifestyle for a number of years. Recently, I walked into the office of a colleague I had worked with seven years prior, before having my two kids. She exclaimed, "Kara! You look great! Two kids later, and you look the same! You're amazing." In fact, earlier that morning, as I was getting dressed and putting my dress pants on, I had been pleased by how nicely my pants were sliding on. They were comfortable, and there was room in the thighs to move.

This was a moment to celebrate! Maybe not to celebrate with a tub of ice cream, but certainly to take some time to relish in the compliment and congratulate myself for the effort I've consistently been putting forth. It doesn't necessarily mean that I've arrived at or come to the end of my journey, but it's a marked point of accomplishment and an occasion to pat myself on the back. Success!

Many people are more than happy to compliment you when you look great. Don't even think for a moment that it's inauthentic. When my partner calls me a MILF, I'm genuinely flattered, and I'm succeeding in my commitment to be a "yummy mommy." It's refreshing to see someone with rosy cheeks, full of energy, and moving freely. It's a presence that people can both see and feel. When people compliment, take it in. Take this as an opportunity to celebrate that you look great. This is the universe's way of sending a reminder to you to relish in the points of accomplishment along your healthy journey.

When we were vacationing in Mexico at the pool one day, my dad and son got out of the water and walked over to where I was laying on a lounge chair. My dad shared with me that my son had just said to him in the pool that I was fat. My dad turned to my son, who was standing in front of us, and said sternly, "Your mom isn't fat. She's trim." I smiled at my dad and said, "It's okay, Dad." Then I asked my son if he was saying that I was fat because my stomach is still fat. He nodded. I said, "You're right. I'm still working on that one Honey." I shared with my dad that we have had conversations at home about me being self-conscious about my tummy.

Although I hadn't yet conquered by tummy, I had made huge progress in my health. In fact, I was remembering what my body looked like 18 months prior, when I had been at that exact same vacation spot in Mexico. I remembered coming back from a walk with a girlfriend and admitting to her with humor, annoyance, and embarrassment that it was uncomfortable to walk around because the fat on my thighs was rubbing and sticking together. My legs were getting hot and sticky and uncomfortable, especially when I was wearing shorts. My girlfriend laughed, admitting that she was surprised and entertained with my frank comment. The flavor of her laughter indicated that she may have been experiencing the same feelings.

When I verbalized my discomfort and embarrassment that day with my girlfriend, I got present to what was true, with no exaggeration, justification, or story. I was carrying more weight than what was physically and emotionally comfortable for me. As I mentioned earlier, I think one key to good health is to be completely honest with how things are and how things aren't. I acknowledged that my thighs were fat and that it was annoying and embarrassing. If you tell yourself lies, nothing will change. Telling yourself the truth is the first step. In that moment, I became even more aware and committed to continuing on my journey of health transformation. I made a choice that I would look great and, most importantly, feel great on my next vacation.

That day at the pool, despite my son's reminder about my tummy still being a work in progress, I was proud of what I had accomplished in the 18 months since the last trip. A number of people (friends and family) had complimented me on how great I looked. As I was walking around on vacation, I felt proud that I could walk comfortably and without sticky thighs rubbing. How I looked and, most importantly, how I felt was a result of many different choices in my diet, hours at the gym, etc. in the 18 months prior. It was all worth it. I felt proud. More than anything, I knew that I had a healthier body. It was something to acknowledge and celebrate.

Be Committed

There are no shortcuts. As I was writing this chapter, an advertisement came on the radio. A swimwear store was pronouncing the three steps to looking great in a swimsuit: 1) go to the store 2) try on a certain brand of swimsuit that tucks everything in, and 3) be impressed with how you look in the suit. Really?! Sounds like a temporary Band-Aid solution and quite likely an expensive Band-Aid solution to me. How about putting that money into exercise classes or organic food or a consult with a naturopath in order to get closer to looking and feeling great in a swimsuit?

Creating health and a healthy lifestyle takes commitment and diligence. It doesn't have to be hard. Parts of it might be. I'm all about taking the easy track when it works, but there are some things that simply require time and effort. Nobody is perfect. I'm certainly not. There have been days when I've eaten French fries in the morning, a big bag of potato chips mid-day, and three ice cream sandwiches late in the afternoon. Sometimes I eat poorly for a few weeks at a time. Then I simply acknowledge that it was a bad day or a bad run and get back on the clean-eating train again.

Enhancing health is about retraining and creating a new normal around health. There are many people in the world who think it's normal to live and walk without shoes. This is what they've learned and grown accustomed to. Believe me, you can learn and grow accustomed to some shifts in lifestyle that will enhance your health. It will take time, and it will take dedication.

This isn't about being obsessed. It's about being committed. When you're committed, you're in control and clear about what your next steps are, what you're diligently working toward, and why. You may decide to eat raw for a year or be a vegetarian for a year. Or you may go on a detox for a month. And those habits may then turn into your lifestyle, one month and one year at a time. We need to always be open to learning new information and ideas to maintain health and open to taking the energy and time to do so. If you have a baby, that may be the most healthful year of your life (because you're off work and have time to eat well and exercise regularly), or it may be the most unhealthful year of your life (because you have three other children to take care of). Whatever the circumstances are in your life, recognize that everything ebbs and flows. What needs to persist is a continued curiosity and interest in health and a continued commitment to enhance it. There is no perfect place to get to in terms of a healthy body and healthy lifestyle.

Believe me: your life, my life, and all of our lives on this planet will be way more chill when we all get committed to caring for our bodies. Health must come first. All the possessions, friends, and time in the world cannot compensate for poor health. When we get connected to this fundamental priority, our mood and our energy shifts. Our ability to connect with and contribute to others skyrockets. Can you imagine a world full of human beings that are healthy and happy because they eat nourishing food, get fresh air and exercise, and rest? What a life that would be for you. What a life that would be for you and me. What a life that would be for the world.

Give Give Give

> "Let us not be satisfied with just giving money. Money is not enough, money can be got, but they need your hearts to love them. So, spread your love everywhere you go."
>
> MOTHER TERESA

Do you give to get—or do you give to give? Webster's Dictionary defines "give" as to "bestow without receiving a return, to confer without compensation." In other words, giving is intended to occur for the sake of giving. A chill and abundant life is full of giving. In any moment of every day, ask yourself, "How can I give?"

There is no beginning or end to the span of giving. Most commonly, giving is associated with giving time and/or money, and often giving to a charitable group. The key thing here is to recognize that giving can become a way of life, a context around which to look at creating life. Giving creates a positive and abundant energy that fills us, the people around us, and the people around those people. It creates happiness and love and uplifts the world.

We can always be looking for ways to give, whether it's holding a door open for someone, helping a child at the playground, buying a product from a giving company, giving a hug, attending a charitable event, etc. Imagine a world where everyone was looking to give to the people around them in every moment. Giving reaps giving.

Give Generously

There have been many times in my life when I had the least but gave the most. At the times when I was worried about the grocery bill as I walked around the supermarket shopping for food for the kids and me, I was most empathetic to those who experience this stress on a regular basis. I was thankful to be at the supermarket and to have the money that I did to buy food. I couldn't even imagine what it would be like to not have the option to go to the supermarket. The kids and I regularly pick up extra items and drop them into the food bank on our way out of the store.

In order to give generously, we need to give up being stingy. In order to give up being stingy, we need to first recognize all of the ways that we are being stingy. What's in the way of you giving? Is it that you think other people should give first? Do you have expectations about what giving should look like? Do you expect something in return when you give? Do you think there will be less for you if you give? Are there times when you just don't feel like giving?

Start catching yourself saying things (whether to yourself or others) that indicate you are being stingy. The things you say may sound something like:

• Do you know how much I've already given?

• Other people have way more to give than me—they should give.

- I don't have time.

- Really? You want/expect more?

- I hate how people just expect handouts.

- That's not who I am.

- Some people are just more fortunate than others. That's the way it is.

- Why should I? Others don't.

- I'm too tired.

- Everywhere I turn, someone is asking for something.

- I work hard. They're lazy. I won't share the fruits of my labor with people who do nothing.

- That's not my responsibility.

- I don't have anything to give.

- I just gave this and that.

- I'm not going to pretend I like giving when I don't.

- Someone who is not so busy can give/do that.

- I don't feel like it.

These aren't thoughts that we're eager to admit to ourselves or others. But believe me, even admitting any flavor of this thinking will give access to a breakthrough in how stingy you're being. Think about any thoughts or excuses you've had recently that have prevented you from giving. In the next few days and weeks, notice what goes on in your head when you get stingy about giving.

Be honest. Reflect on all of the ways you're being stingy about giving. Also think about the underlying reasons why you're being stingy.

What are your negative beliefs or judgments around giving?

_____

_____

_____

_____

_____

There are many, many people who work in giving professions. There are teachers, health care professionals, child care providers, social workers, counsellors, alternative health providers, mediators, career planners, and many other helping professionals. In fact, most people contribute to society in their work or business. There are cashiers, engineers, construction workers, administrative professionals, electricians, etc.

Catch yourself if you have a notion that when you're done work, you're done giving. It may sound something like, "I've done my part, now my time is my time," or "Do you know what I already give in my work?" I acknowledge that it is a huge commitment to contribute at work—and also to contribute to family and friends outside of work. Still, I absolutely encourage you to look beyond. There doesn't need to be an end to our giving. We're never off duty from giving.

Some people put quotas on their giving. What they say to themselves may sound something like, "I volunteer for two organizations already, so I'm not going to give blood, too." A common example of a quota that people put on giving is that they put a certain percentage or amount of their income toward a cause on an ongoing basis. Some people (not all) look at this as their primary giving focus and decline giving in other ways. A quota can put a cap on giving not only in the area where the quota is set, but also in other areas. For instance, if someone is committed to giving 10 percent to a cause, perhaps s/he could easily give 15 percent to the cause. This person doesn't, however, because they don't see that they can because of the fixation on the 10 percent. And, if there is a commitment to give 10 percent to a cause, there may be a tendency to not give in other areas and in other ways— perhaps justifying that s/he is already giving a set amount on a regular basis to a cause.

Random acts of kindness are wonderful. They too can limit generosity. The challenge with random acts of kindness is that they're often thought of as something people do once in a blue moon. If someone does a random act of kindness, they post it on Facebook, get acknowledgment, and then wait for the next blue moon to do another random act of kindness. Random acts of kindness can be done all day, every day. They're often actions that aren't time or energy intensive. They're actions that don't require public acknowledgement. For example:

- picking up garbage and throwing it in the trash;

- holding a door open;

- wiping the counter of a public washroom dry;

- offering to help someone carry or load something;

- helping a child with a task if her/his parent is busy;

- picking a recyclable item out of the trash and recycling it;

- giving someone a few coins to complete their purchase or so they don't have to dig in their wallet;

- letting someone go ahead of you in line;

- holding a baby while a mom does something;

- doing some weeding in a community garden;

- plugging a parking meter that has expired; and

- informing a manager of someone's outstanding work performance.

There are endless ideas for random acts of kindness. We simply need to start paying attention to what people around us may need help with in any given moment to see what would make a difference. Let's stop being stingy and putting caps on random acts of kindness. Let's all do random acts of kindness all day, every day.

One of the biggest tests in giving generously is having the eagerness to give, even when it's not noticed, acknowledged, or appreciated. Giving to anyone, at any time, with no expectation of anything in return is a demonstration of pure unconditional love for self and others.

For some of you, I am preaching to the choir. I acknowledge you for who you are. You're constantly being generous, always looking for ways to give. You walk around this planet giving, giving, giving. You're always thinking of others, speaking positively of them, giving gifts whether small or large, being generous with your time, doing random acts of kindness, supporting organizations that are built on giving, and the list goes on and on and on. Nonetheless, for you people, too, please do a double check and still look at ways that you may be being stingy and putting caps on your giving.

For everyone, let's take a good look again and let's consider the following:

• Do you assume that giving has to be in the way of money or time?

• Do you only give when it'll be seen and when you'll receive acknowledgment?

• Are you only generous to a certain kind of person?

• Do you keep track of who you've given to and where your relationship is at (who has given more)?

• Do you only believe in giving to family, or do you only believe in giving to people who aren't family?

• Even when you think you're giving unconditionally, is there a hint of expecting something in return?

• Will you offer to give or do you wait for people to ask?

There's certainly no right or wrong amounts or ways to give, but I do believe that we need to continually consider how we may be unconsciously limiting our giving. Whatever level of giving seems generous in your life right now can be challenged. We can all up our antes. We have no idea what we're capable of until we're open and committed to expand.

I attended a charity event some time ago and was struck by what giving generously and going above and beyond can look like. Not only did Wayne Lee, an international speaker, donate his time to do his presentation, but he also included a free DVD program in each of the gift bags for the event participants. (While the other speakers at the event also donated their time to do the presentations, they sold their products after they had finished speaking.) Lee also spent hours upon hours organizing the event. I have a feeling there are many other ways in which he gave to the event, and continually gives to this organization. Few people in the room probably noticed or were aware of the level of his generosity. This is not the point. It doesn't matter. Lee went above and beyond. I've learned that this is who he is on an ongoing basis.

Give Without Obligation

Many people give because they feel they should or want to avoid the feeling of guilt they feel if they don't give. Many people also give because they think they need to return a favor or return something of the equivalent that was given to them. This is giving out of obligation, and there is a lack of authenticity and freedom around this kind of giving.

When, where, and how have you given out of obligation recently?

_____

_____

_____

_____

_____

_____

Surround Yourself with Giving

Whether it's your friends, the companies you support, the community you live in, consider how you can align yourself with people, organizations, and a lifestyle that's oriented toward giving. The decisions you make every day will take you closer to, or further from, this commitment. The stronger your choice and actions are to surround yourself by giving, the more that you'll start to see generosity unfolding naturally all around you.

Over the years, as I've determined that giving is a clear commitment in my life, my networks and lifestyle have shifted. It's not an accident that the moms in my circle of friends have offered to look after my kids if there's ever a time when I need to get something done. It's not an accident that my friends give their time to charities, work for charitable groups, and fundraise for charity. It's not an accident that friends refer clients to me. It's not an accident that there's always someone to call if I need a piece of furniture moved. It's not an accident that my friends organize block parties in their neighborhoods. It's not an accident that I experience people holding open doors for me, helping my kids when we're out, and doing special favors for me when giving me service. It's not an accident that friends offer me free tickets to events. It's not an accident that my colleagues are creating socially conscious businesses. I experience being surrounded by giving because I've made it a priority to give and have surrounded myself with giving folk.

We create our own reality. There's a fable about a person who's thinking of moving to another place and asks a wise resident of the new potential place, "How are people there?" The wise person responds, "Well, that depends. How are the people where you are?"

Our experience of life is in line with how we create it to be. The energy of giving is positive and abundant. When we choose to focus on giving to others, to ourselves, and to worthy causes, we make it known in our communication, in our actions, and in our energy that this is how we're choosing to live.

When we get off track, we can bring ourselves back on track. We can catch ourselves when we're focused on taking, judging others for taking, or having the experience of someone taking from us. We can notice when we get weird in any way about giving or receiving—for instance, when we have a story about what a person should do or say for us to give to them, or we have an expectation about what and how someone should give to us. Giving is a pure, beautiful act of human spirit and generosity. When there are expectations, judgments, conditions, or anything of this sort, we need to catch ourselves in this weird energy and bring ourselves back to what giving is really about. We can remind ourselves that our commitment is to focus on giving, and the positivity and abundance around that.

We can all work together to create synergy and a new world of givers. We can encourage and inspire our children, friends, family, colleagues, and acquaintances to all work together and create a world of givers. We can shift from being skeptical and thinking that people only give to get, to being trusting and believing that people have good hearts. We can become a world where all people love each other as neighbors and are eager to give the shirt off their backs in any given moment. There may be people who don't choose this path and stay in the negative energy, but eventually, with a real shift, the people living in light and abundance will envelope the rest. This shift in thinking can be created just by choosing this path.

Give in Meaningful Ways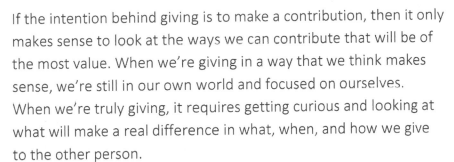

If the intention behind giving is to make a contribution, then it only makes sense to look at the ways we can contribute that will be of the most value. When we're giving in a way that we think makes sense, we're still in our own world and focused on ourselves. When we're truly giving, it requires getting curious and looking at what will make a real difference in what, when, and how we give to the other person.

Gary Chapman's work, *The 5 Love Languages: How to Express Heartfelt Commitment to Your Mate*, offers significant insight into purposeful ways that we can give to each other. He identifies five love languages: words of affirmation, physical touch, quality time, acts of service, and gifts. He explains how people have different preferences for how they receive affection and appreciation. People generally have one primary love language and a secondary love language. *The 5 Languages of Appreciation in the Workplace: Empowering Organizations by Encouraging People*, written by Chapman and Paul White, outlines the preferences people have for acknowledgment in a work setting. Where some people would rather receive a compliment or verbal praise, others may prefer to receive a reward or a gift. Like anything, you can enhance your ability to identify people's preferences and express love and appreciation in relevant ways with practice. In fact, the biggest hint in knowing what will most resonate with someone else is to look at the ways that they most often express their love and appreciation.

Words of affirmation and compliments are powerful. In watching some dating videos put out by Matthew Hussey, I was struck by his comment that people, in general, are stingy with compliments. This is so true. Giving a compliment is something that takes little time and effort, and yet we're generally stingy about giving them. Hussey emphasized in one of his videos that when you say a compliment with enthusiasm and authenticity, it can really be an enlivening and memorable moment for the other person. Compliments are easy to give when they're authentic. They support us in looking for the things that we appreciate about people. Compliments fill our cups when we give them and other people's cups when they receive them. Verbal and written compliments can become a habit and way of living as you practice giving them throughout your days.

I find physical touch to be an interesting love language. My son and daughter are both very touchy, but this is not my go-to love language. In fact, there are times when I catch myself being annoyed by physical touch or even trying to brush it off. (No, this is not something I like to admit.) I need to constantly remind myself that physical touch is something that my kids, and other people in my life, need from me. Whether it's a handshake, hug, high-five, hand on the shoulder, or back rub, some people long for this physical connection. If this isn't one of your primary languages, you may notice it feels like these people regularly infringe on your personal space. Remember that by opening up to this language and practicing it, you're giving a precious gift of sharing love and appreciation.

Since time is the most precious resource we have on this planet, giving our time is one of the most meaningful ways we can give. Giving your time is a love language and a true expression of commitment and kindness, whether you're giving seconds, minutes, hours, or days of your time. Take a few extra minutes not to rush a phone call. Pick something up that someone has dropped or walked away from and return it to them. Go out with a friend who you know is experiencing challenges in her/his life. Spend a break at work hanging out with a colleague. Visit someone who is sick. Offer to assist in setting up for an event that a non-profit organization is organizing. Plant and care for some flowers in a public space in your neighborhood. Volunteer at a school.

Thank other people for their time when they spend it with you. Don't expect or take for granted that people need to take time to be with you. The more we acknowledge the value of other people's time and appreciate when they're assisting us, playing with us, supporting us, encouraging us, waiting for us, working with us, or serving us, the more we'll be conscious of the gift of time and also want to give our time to others. It will create an awareness of the difference that people spending quality, focused time with each other makes.

One paradox I've experienced is that the more generously I give my time, the more time seems to expand. I used to think—and still catch myself thinking on occasion—that there is only so much time in the day and that I need to be strategic and efficient with my time. This is true to some extent. The reality is that time is finite. However, as I nurture and foster relationships by giving my time and attention generously, I find that with the connectedness and community I create around me, more and more things take care of themselves and don't need to get done. For example, there's less drama and conflict to deal with. I spend less time looking for people, such as a good handyman, because someone I know mentions a good handyman in conversation. Rather than spending time marketing in my business, clients naturally fall into my lap as friends and colleagues refer people to me because they respect the relationship we've developed. People I know offer to help me with things that need to get done without me asking, or they're more than happy to help if I do ask them.

When people choose to spend time alone, they're robbing others of the opportunity to experience the precious gift of sharing time together. There may be a tendency to think that there's no impact of spending time alone—that no interaction with other people would mean that there's no impact on other people at all. But there is an impact. Relationships and community are not created—or cease to exist—as people spend more and more time alone. Because connectedness and relationships are what make this world go 'round, there's an impact when the energy and love on this planet aren't expanded.

It's worth learning about Chapman's work on the languages of love, and Chapman's and White's work on the languages of appreciation. They certainly offer many practical insights and tips on all five languages. Given that you now know full well that there are different languages of love and appreciation, and that they resonate differently with people, consider it an essential life skill in creating love and happiness to be aware of how these languages play out.

Give by Receiving

As I was writing this chapter, I became connected to how we can give by being receptive to others' giving. Pushing away offers of support doesn't work for the person offering the support, and it doesn't work for the person who could've received the support. This is an idea that may seem counterintuitive: we give by receiving.

I recently offered a ride to the airport to someone. I received a text reply that read, "I think I'll just cab it. It's an early flight LOL." I felt disappointed, annoyed, and cheated. Not outraged, but peeved. I wouldn't have offered the ride if I didn't want to drive to the airport, even if it was at 3 or 4 a.m. It was a gift I was happy to give. I wanted to spend time with this person.

It can be a leap of faith to trust that other people are giving generously and authentically. There is a tendency to assume that people are giving out of obligation, pity, or otherwise, which creates resistance in us. We need to receive in the same that way we are committed to give—generously and authentically. In other words, rather than think that someone offered something just to be nice, or because they thought they should, or because they felt sorry for you, or because they want something in return, push yourself to believe that the person offered out of the pure goodness of their heart. Even if you're still questioning their true intentions, give the benefit of the doubt and commit to believing in the purity of the offer. This can be a real shift.

If I had offered to give the ride to the airport out of obligation, I would've been relieved that the offer was declined. But I didn't. I genuinely wanted to help and connect. There's nothing wrong with taking a cab and there's nothing wrong with accepting a ride from someone. They are two different choices. By choosing to receive giving, you open your heart and create an opportunity for connectedness, relationship, and community.

Choose to give up any negative and limiting story that you have that stops you from receiving. Perhaps it's a story that you're only strong if you do things yourself, or that you're not good enough for people to care that much, or that you don't want to be a burden on others, or that only lazy people accept help. Be honest. You have a story. Whatever it is, give it up. People want to give to you, and you're being caught up in yourself by not allowing them to.

When and how do you resist receiving?

_____

_____

_____

_____

_____

_____

_____

Receiving openly is a practice. I've recently been repeating the affirmation, "I am open to receiving anything from anyone at anytime," throughout the day. Then I practice. The other day, my daughter handed me $100 when we were playing Monopoly. She said, "Here, Mom, this is for you." I responded, "Oh, you keep it Sweetie. Thank you." Yes, I still need to practice.

Give to Yourself

What I hear over and over from people, especially when they're stressed, is that they neglect to care for themselves. They quickly and easily get caught up in trying to be everything to everyone and forget that they're someone, too. They become immersed in drama and circumstances and allow a fog to surround them. The irony is that when we're most stressed, we need self-care the most, but this is the first thing that goes out the window. We don't eat, sleep, exercise, socialize, drink water, or relax adequately.

Giving to yourself is a foundation for peace, happiness, and success. We need to start making sure that we put the priority of giving to ourselves at least at the same level as other things. Putting self-care at a higher level of priority would be even better, but let's start with first steps for those who currently have self-care as their lowest priority. This means scheduling in time for exercise and giving it the same level of commitment as a lunch with a family member, business meeting, or appointment at the bank. It means that money is spent on things like personal development, massage, and good food. You are your most important resource and asset, so prioritize accordingly.

The area of self-care should not be the first and primary place to look when cutting spending and time. On a budget, perhaps there isn't the money to pay a personal coach hundreds or thousands of dollars, but there may be an affordable online seminar or teleclass that would offer significant learning. (Register now at www.karaderinger.com.) Yes, choices need to be made, but we can use our creativity. Perhaps there is a coupon for a local massage business or a massage school that offers discounted massage services because their students are practicing on clients. Perhaps a friend can come over for a glass of iced tea or a cold beer while you take care of a chore or project that can be done while you visit (maybe even with her/his help). Get innovative! Also consider that spending money on self-care, such as hundreds or thousands of dollars in personal development, will be the best investment you ever make.

Make sure you're making arrangements in your life to ensure that your needs are met. One thing my mom said to me years ago was, "You need to get a babysitter." I could see that she was committed to me having lots of supports in place in order to take care of myself. Another thing I do is hire people to take care of things around the house if I'm short on time. If I have a choice between buying a new outfit and cleaning the house myself or paying a cleaner for a few hours so that I have time to go exercise, I choose the latter.

Creating structures to meet your needs means looking at your life and identifying what gets in the way of you taking care of yourself and finding a resource or a solution so that you can and will take care of yourself. Structures create new freedom and accountability. For instance, joining a mastermind group or book club or networking group creates a commitment where you get out of the house with the intention of fulfilling a need that's important to you in your life. If you're running in circles and wasting time trying to keep track of commitments and apologizing and making up for missed commitments, use the calendar in your phone, a daytimer, virtual assistant, or any other method to organize your schedule and be more efficient with your time. Hiring a babysitter, gardener, bookkeeper, or housecleaner on a weekly or biweekly basis creates room in your schedule to fulfill your personal needs. Blocking off time in your calendar creates a visible commitment.

It's also important to generate support all around you to ensure your needs are met. Share with the people in your life what's important to you and why and how they can help you. I've had many conversations with the kids at home to explain that I have needs and responsibilities and that I need their support in this. I'll say, "I need you to please go to bed. I'm tired, too. And I have my exercises and work to get done tonight. So the later you stay up, the later I need to stay up. Can you help me, please?" Now that my kids are a bit older, sometimes I actually take a 20-minute nap during the day while they play. I let them know that I'm tired and that I'm going to lay down for a 20-minute nap. They're usually quick and excited to get me one of their blankets and a pillow and snuggle me in. I set my alarm, and they're fine to play for 20 minutes. This teaches them that I have needs, too.

No one likes being in the company of a martyr. When you give and give and give to others and complain about there being nothing left for you, you're not doing anyone any favors or being a hero. You're just self-sabotaging and being grumpy. Stop it. You're not going to get any medals of honor for putting yourself last, so stop doing it.

Self-care must be a commitment. We need our physical and mental health in order to contribute to others. Put the oxygen mask on yourself first. Identify the critical things that fill your cup. They're different for everyone, so really look at the things that give you juice. Granted, you may not be able to have and do all of them, but do ensure that you're continually looking at how to nurture yourself. Only when our own cup is full will it spill over to uplift others.

Give Creatively

Each of us tends to have our own set of ideas around what's possible to give, and this collection of ideas has emerged out of the totality of our life experience. Yet rarely do we challenge ourselves to look past what we already know is possible in the way of giving. We often focus on what we can't do, saying we don't have enough time to take that on, or it's not in our budget to give that much money, or our schedule doesn't allow for us to commit to that day. We don't always take a lot of time or use a lot of creativity to really think about what and how we can give.

Openness to give, plus some creativity, can produce beautiful results. A friend of mine shared recently that she discovered that a chain retail location in our city had approximately 200 beautiful holiday ornaments leftover that they needed to either donate or throw away. Because the ornaments had the markings of the previous year on them, they were no longer sellable. The ornaments were individually wrapped in boxes and had a regular ticket price of about $20. My amazing friend had a brainwave and got together a group of friends. They spent an afternoon—about five hours—gluing decals on the holiday balls to cover the markings of the year. They donated the beautifully decorated ornaments to a local children's hospital to sell as a fundraiser. Even at a sale price of 40 percent below the original retail price ($12 each), they stood to raise $2,400. Talk about giving. These are items that would've ended up in the landfill. These ladies kept the ornaments from the landfill and supported a children's hospital with five hours of their time.

There are many everyday occasions and extraordinary causes to give time to, so if one opportunity doesn't fit, there's likely another that does. My aunt used to volunteer to cuddle and hold babies at the hospital. A friend of mine volunteered at a soup kitchen. Some people spend a night driving people safely home from holiday parties as a fundraiser for a charitable group. My mom volunteers to set up the meditation labyrinth at her spiritual center. I offer to look after people's children so they can connect as a couple or get something done (like packing for a move). In many ways, volunteering your time can be more powerful than giving money. For instance, you can contribute to organizing or working at a charitable event that generates large volumes of funds. Look around and pick your flavor. Where would you love to give your time?

Open up your eyes to new ways of giving in all ways. Get creative in how you can give in ways that you had never thought of before. Reading this chapter will likely create some new openings for you to start noticing creative ways that you can give. Give in ways that fill your cup too, so that you're in the space of multiplying the happiness and love.

Give by Being Grateful

It's no mystery that gratitude expressed aloud is uplifting and contagious. While people don't always expect a thank you, they certainly appreciate it. If someone is generous enough to give to you in any way, it's the least you can do to notice it and acknowledge it. People respect and admire others who consistently show gratitude for how things are and what they have, rather than complaining about what they wish things would be and what they don't have. When you say thank you for anything and everything, you're encouraging people to continue contributing. Whether they contribute to you directly, or indirectly, your acknowledgment creates a positive energy that invites more contribution into your life.

One thing I'm incredibly grateful for is that my parents taught me to notice the kinds of things that other people do and to say thank you. It's wonderful to be in the habit of saying thank you no matter how small or big the thing that you're thanking the other person for is. I've taken on this practice with my children. The other day, as my son was strapping himself in the car to leave from a going-away pizza party that some friends were hosting, I asked, "Did you thank them for dinner?" My son responded, "Yes." I frowned and said, "I don't think you did, Honey. Please go do that." He sighed. "Really mom?" he said. I said, "Yes, really." He unstrapped his belt, walked back up the sidewalk to the door, and knocked. He said his thank you, and I could hear the host and other parents cooing, "Aw," as he expressed his gratitude.

Sometimes I'm reminded of the importance of being grateful when I have an experience of someone else not being grateful of something I've given. For example, a few months ago, I took some time to write a quick feedback note to a local yoga studio that I'd begun frequenting, as it's a fairly new establishment. I wanted to be of service and to share some information that I thought they may not be aware of and that could be helpful. I have a belief that the gift of my time in the form of feedback can contribute to enhancing the quality of business and services for everyone's benefit and to raise the bar for how business is done. Business owners and staff aren't always aware of what would make a positive difference, so it's a gift to share information that supports them in making positive changes.

Here's the email I sent to the yoga studio:
I'm new to the studio and enjoyed my first class this week. In one class, I overheard a lady saying that she likes the studio but has found a lot of shifting with instructors. She'd like more consistency and stability with the instructors. Thought I'd pass on this feedback in case you don't hear it via another channel.

Here's the response I received:
Hi Kara,
Thank you for bringing this to my concern. We do our best to keep consistency, but often stuff happens and we have to switch schedules around, e.g., teachers becoming pregnant, getting different job positions, etc. We also do like to change it up and keep the schedule fresh by switching teachers around.

In the response, I heard explanation and justifying. The response was written as if this was my concern. Perhaps I didn't spell out clearly enough in my message that the purpose of the note was just an FYI for the sake of enhancing business, and that I didn't personally have a concern. Nonetheless, I had taken time out of my life to share this information with the intention of being in service, and there seemed to be little appreciation in the response.

Here's the response I would've liked to receive:
Thank you very much for your email, Kara. We really appreciate you taking the time to share this feedback with us. Feedback is always a great way to learn how to improve, so we'll certainly take this into consideration. Thank you for choosing our studio for your yoga practice.

We're not naturally grateful for all feedback. It's probable that, in the face of negative feedback, we will get defensive, even when the other person has an intention to be helpful with the information they are sharing with us. We can even get defensive about positive feedback. When I'm reacting negatively to something or someone, and know that I'm not in the space of being grateful, I give some time and space before I respond in order to allow gratitude to creep into the picture. Sometimes it takes minutes for gratitude to creep in. Sometimes it takes hours. Sometimes it takes days or weeks. When gratitude is authentically present, I re-engage in the conversation or situation.

When a colleague graciously accepted an invitation to do an interview with me, she suggested a Skype session instead of a phone call. I could feel some annoyance and resistance when I read her message suggesting the Skype session because Skype was not a format that I was familiar with. My schedule was packed and I didn't have a lot of time to figure something new out. When I noticed my own irritation, I waited to respond to her message until the following day. She had agreed to generously give her time for the interview and the last thing I wanted to do was be irritable and ungrateful with her. The next day, I began to recognize that my colleague was suggesting Skype because she really wanted us to capture the full value of the interview by recording the session. I was grateful for her creativity and her commitment to quality. My response the next day communicated my appreciation to her, and I suggested that we do a phone call with me using my recorder to capture our session. She happily agreed.

Always look for things to appreciate about people and acknowledge them for. The biggest gift you can give someone is acknowledging them for something they didn't even know that they were giving. For instance, if something someone said inspired you to take action, let them know that they made a difference in your life. Or if they gave you a gift some time ago and you think of them when you're enjoying it, let them know how you still appreciate the gift. When you highlight how people have touched you and contributed to you, then they become moved by the positive impact of their own giving. You're moved, they're moved, and both of you are more likely to continue giving generously in the world.

Be grateful for everything. Take nothing for granted. Be grateful for the time that people take to talk to you. Be grateful for the sunshine. Be grateful for the people who let you into traffic. Be grateful for clean laundry. Be grateful for the person who delivers your mail. In any moment, look for what there is to be grateful for. Louise Hay talks about being grateful for the bills we need to pay because they show that someone was generous enough to offer us services in advance and in good faith, trusting that we would pay for them. We can focus on being grateful for the money we have to pay for bills. Make it a habit and commitment to be grateful for anything and everything.

On the first day of spring, the kids and I were shoveling two feet of heavy wet snow off of the driveway onto the yard. After many, many months of cold and snow, the last thing we wanted to do was deal with a particularly wet and heavy snowfall on the driveway. As we shoveled and panted, I said, "Well, the good thing about this is that the snow is going to melt, and it's going to water our grass. This is perfect for spring."

Give in the Economy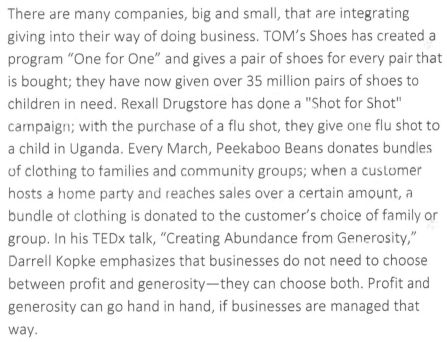

There are many companies, big and small, that are integrating giving into their way of doing business. TOM's Shoes has created a program "One for One" and gives a pair of shoes for every pair that is bought; they have now given over 35 million pairs of shoes to children in need. Rexall Drugstore has done a "Shot for Shot" campaign; with the purchase of a flu shot, they give one flu shot to a child in Uganda. Every March, Peekaboo Beans donates bundles of clothing to families and community groups; when a customer hosts a home party and reaches sales over a certain amount, a bundle of clothing is donated to the customer's choice of family or group. In his TEDx talk, "Creating Abundance from Generosity," Darrell Kopke emphasizes that businesses do not need to choose between profit and generosity—they can choose both. Profit and generosity can go hand in hand, if businesses are managed that way.

The opposite of giving is taking, and many businesses take from communities, the environment, their employees, and so on. It doesn't take a lot of research or observation to identify which businesses are taking. From coffee to housecleaning to any other product or service, there's an element of responsibility on the part of the consumer to seek out companies that are oriented toward giving, rather than taking and destroying.

Kopke points out that Apple's microprocessors and wiring are made from coltan, a metallic ore mined in the Democratic Republic of Congo (DRC). He states that about 90 percent of the mines in the DRC are controlled by militia groups, which kidnap small children and arm them so they can kill other children. In other words, buying Apple products supports the perpetuation of child soldiers in the DRC. My stomach turns as I look at the iPhone and iPad sitting in front of me right now. I had no idea what went into the Apple products at the time of purchasing them.

Some companies give things to their customers, which is just marketing, not giving. Further, what they give sometimes lacks integrity (environmentally friendly, healthy, etc.) One day, I tried to return a box of free Halloween candy that I had received at a large grocery store chain for spending over a certain amount on my groceries. The clerk informed me that I couldn't return the free item. There isn't a choice in the free item. It is what it is and no cash refunds or credits would be given. She explained to me that when they give a free turkey as the free item, some customers object to the turkey, saying that they're vegetarian. The clerk said there's nothing they can do. The vegetarian customers can't even donate the turkey to the food bank because it's a perishable item. The clerk recommended that I donate my Halloween candy to the food bank. I shared with her that I'm happy to donate to the food bank but that candy isn't food in my eyes. One summer week, the free item for this same large grocery chain was a cooler. As I passed the mountainous display of coolers in the store that week, I could just picture that same heap of coolers in the landfill. I'm fundamentally opposed to a company giving free items to their customers when the items aren't practical or lack integrity. This is not giving.

We can speak out and verbally express our desire for companies to be responsible and creative in their approaches and practices. Over a year ago, my friend started a power company. When we met for coffee, I asked if the power services arc based on green energy. He went into a lengthy explanation about how the technology in green power sources is not what it needs to be and how the availability of green power is limited. I emphasized that I was currently doing some research into making sure my power supplier is a company aligned with some form of green energy. A year later, I met my friend at a local green networking event. He shared with me how his company is implementing a green energy option for consumers. I'm sure the process of moving in this direction as a company was not a quick or straight one, but I do believe that I contributed in some small way to planting the seeds for this to unfold.

Whether it's a local business or international business, we can vote with our dollars by supporting companies that are oriented toward giving. Let's look at how they're mindful of their production practices, marketing and promotions, profit sharing, employee development, etc. On the flip side, of course, this can also look like choosing not to align with people and organizations that are oriented to taking and destroying. Look at the restaurant you're choosing to eat at, the clothing you choose to buy, the utility company you sign on with, the charity you donate to, and all the other choices you make in where you align and support. Be mindful of what that organization stands for and how they operate. If it's a choice between a local eatery that uses eco-friendly takeout containers versus a corporate eatery that uses Styrofoam containers, choose the first. If you're a business owner, make public your commitment to responsibility and generosity so that consumers can choose to align with your organization. Each of us has power to make choices in what organizations we support and align with. Simple choices, especially when multiplied by many people, can lead to powerful changes. This is how personal and world transformation occurs.

Give In to Tao

My most major shift in life around giving was inspired by Wayne Dyer. In his book *Change Your Thoughts—Change Your Life: Living the Wisdom of the Tao*, Dyer discusses how to live simply, peacefully, and generously. In one particular chapter in the book, Dyer tells a story of giving one of his most treasured possessions, a watch, as a gift. He declares that when we give away an item that is precious to us, we experience true feelings of letting go, freedom, and joy. The more precious the item, the stronger the feelings of letting go, freedom, and joy are—which is counterintuitive for most of us. When we learn to let go of something that we think makes us happy, we can feel at a gut and heart level what really creates happiness.

When I was first listening to his book on CD (this is generally how I "read"), I took a first step in testing out Dyer's theory. One day, as I was getting dressed, I put on one of my favorite pink tops, with a beaded pink and purple necklace that I always wore with it. It was like the shirt and necklace were meant for each other. As I started clasping the necklace, I remembered that a friend had commented on the necklace once and said it was beautiful. She had shared that she would love to wear more jewelry, but that wearing jewelry was out of her comfort zone. I responded by saying that I think jewelry supports women in expressing ourselves and in getting in touch with our femininity. I finished clasping the necklace around my neck and decided that this would be the last day I would wear it. I gave the necklace to my girlfriend the next time I saw her. Admittedly, there have been times as I lay my eyes on that pink top in my closet when I wonder if my girlfriend likes the necklace as much as I still do. But I remind myself that it doesn't matter. What matters most is that I think of her fondly every time I put that pink top on now and look for a necklace to wear with it.

When I was really, really ready for a breakthrough experience in the feelings of letting go, freedom, and joy, I decided to ante up and release a large, beloved possession. As I continued to listen to Dyer's book, I inquired with myself about which of my possessions was the most ego driven for me. It didn't take long for me to put my finger on it: my Volkswagen Touareg had a whole bunch of ego wrapped up in it.

The first vehicle I owned was a Volkswagen Beetle. I loved how solid and powerful that car felt on the road. It handled beautifully, and it looked beautiful. It was a metallic bluish purple. Let's just say I wasn't the most careful driver at that time, so I loved that the Beetle was solid and held up like a tank when I bumped into things. When I became pregnant with our first child, I knew that the two doors and small trunk were not going to work with a baby seat and a stroller. For months, I held onto the hope that I wouldn't have to part with my Bug.

When I was about eight months pregnant, my ex-husband and I were both working full-time, selling our home, living with my in-laws, and looking for a new home. There was a lot going on. I made a quick decision to replace my Beetle with the Pontiac Vibe that my mother in-law was selling. It was an easy decision—no research, test drives, or price shopping. It seemed like a good, reliable, practical vehicle. But within a few weeks of driving it, I decided I despised the Vibe. I found it noisy on the road, difficult to handle, and it seemed like it would crumple in an accident with a precious baby on board.

I began looking at a vehicle to replace the Vibe when my son was a few months old. Buying a safe and sturdy SUV seemed to be the sensible answer. After some test driving, I fell in love with a six-year-old BMW X5. It was like driving my Beetle. It rode and handled beautifully. The problem I discovered was that my ex-husband wouldn't have any part of having a BMW parked in our driveway. He saw it as a status symbol. I kept looking at SUVs and fell in love with the Volkswagen Touareg. I thought, "Ha! It rides and handles like the BMW X5, except there's a VW symbol on the hood. He'll go for this one!" It seemed like the perfect solution. I found a great deal on a pre-owned Touareg out of province, and my gracious in-laws drove it home for me. I loved, loved, loved that Touareg. When my mom first got in it one evening, she looked at the front dashboard and said, "It's like I'm in an airplane." The Touareg rode like an airplane. Smooth as silk.

As I was contemplating Dyer's book, I'm not going to lie: I was resisting the idea that my life would be enhanced if I parted with my Touareg, one of my most favorite material possessions. The idea that I would be happier without my Touareg was very hard to comprehend. I knew of the notion that simplicity brings peace and happiness, but I had never truly given something of my own up. I had backpacked through Southeast Asia with my parents as a teen, and had certainly experienced the peace and happiness of simplicity on that five-month trip. But in my adult life, I had been on a path to accumulate more and more. There was a deep part of me that was intrigued by what Dyer was encouraging.

Then one day I went to purchase a new windshield wiper for my Touareg. I visited the dealership, asked for a wiper, and the sales person advised me that the total would be $80. I said, "Oh no, that's okay. I don't need a set of wipers. I just need one." The sales person confirmed, yes, that was the price for one wiper. Like the gas, oil changes, brake jobs (yes a few brake jobs in the span of a few years), and all parts and services for the Touareg, the wipers were extraordinarily costly. Well, perhaps it was time to let go of the Touareg. This definitely helped with my decision. It felt like the universe was speaking.

Guess what I bought to replace the Touareg? No, not a Pontiac Vibe! I went with a Mazda 3 hatchback, and for those of you who know cars, you may say these two models are pretty darn similar. As I was signing the papers to trade the Touareg for the Mazda 3, I was texting my dad with anxiousness and doubt. I was worried I was going to regret the decision. He said, "Don't worry. The first time you fill up for gas at the pumps, you'll know you did the right thing." He was right. The Mazda 3 is everything we need—four doors to haul kids and a hatchback to haul kid stuff and even furniture. (I've squeezed in a twin mattress in the Mazda 3 hatchback on one occasion and a wardrobe on another occasion.) Not only that, but I pushed myself to let go of a major ego-driven object in my life. It was a turning point, and there was a landslide in letting go of all kinds of possessions in the following weeks, months, and years.

I began to feel lighter and happier as I let go of thing after thing after thing. Every week, I would look around my home for things we weren't using. Household objects, clothing, you name it. Stuff began to move out the door on a continual basis. I took donations to Goodwill stores, listed things in the online classified ads, gave gifts. The more that cleared out, the more physical and mental space I enjoyed. The experience of letting go, freedom, and joy is absolutely incredible. I highly recommend it. Just do it.

It may be that you could easily do without jewelry or a vehicle, but look at what you're attached to in the way of material possessions in your life. Take on an experiment of your own to let go and to flow with the experience that comes with letting go. Go ahead and have some fun. Pick one of your big ego objects to part with! When we experience the freedom that giving something up creates, and train ourselves to live this way, there is more freedom to give to others.

Create a Giving Day

Do an experiment. Commit to making one day soon a giving day. Go about your day. Do what you normally do. Don't completely set aside your own priorities and activities throughout the day. Simply engage in the responsibilities and activities of the day as usual. But go about your day in a different way.

Give in every moment and at every opportunity that you can. Let someone into the traffic lane you are in. Text a compliment or encouragement. Lend an empathetic ear. Smile at a homeless person and wish her/him a good day. Allow a parent with children to move ahead of you in line at the supermarket. Give someone a pat on the back or a hug. Thank a service provider. Acknowledge a family member. Send a small gift to someone. Hold the elevator door. Treat yourself to a bubble bath.

Prior to your giving day, spend time daydreaming about how you will give. Think about all the languages of love and how you can express giving to the different people you cross paths with in the day. Notice how other people give as they go about their day. Do a quick Internet search on ideas for random acts of kindness. Even daydreaming about giving will put you in a warm, positive, and loving mood.

What will you do on your giving day? How will you give to others? How will you give to yourself? In what ways will you contribute to creating a more giving economy? What will you give up?

_____

_____

_____

_____

_____

_____

_____

_____

_____

Following the giving day, dedicate some time to give to yourself. Relish in how the giving day went and how it felt. How does it feel in your body? How does it feel in your heart? What were your thoughts throughout the day? What were your feelings? What was challenging? What new commitments can you make for giving in the future? (The key here is to focus on you rather than the reactions—positive or negative—of other people.) Go for a nature walk, paint your nails, meditate, weed the garden, or do some other relaxing activity to ground yourself in the positive energy within and around you.

My Giving Day:

_____

_____

_____

_____

_____

_____

_____

_____

_____

_____

_____

Consider that every day could be a giving day. This is not actually a revolutionary concept. It's a matter of forming some new habits and taking on a new perspective. Giving can become a way of life if this is the choice that's made. It doesn't have to take heaps of time, money, or energy. Simply making small choices on an ongoing basis with the intention of being positive, thoughtful, and generous can create a life where every day is a giving day.

What will you do going forward to create a giving lifestyle?

_____

_____

_____

_____

_____

_____

_____

_____

Here is a passage from Dyer's book *Change Your Thoughts—Change Your Life*:

> "Let go of evaluating yourself on the basis of how much you've accomplished and what is in your financial portfolio. Stop putting a dollar value on all that you have and do. Let go of your need to get a 'good deal' and choose instead to be a being of sharing. You'll be happily surprised by how nice it feels to simply change your belief that you're only successful if you're making money. The less you focus on making a profit—instead shifting your energy to living your purpose in harmony with everyone else—the more money will flow to you and the more opportunities for generosity will be available to you." (page 91)

Go Green

"Environmentalism isn't a discipline or specialty. It's a way of seeing our place in the world. And we need everybody to see the world that way. Don't think 'In order to make a difference, I have to become an environmentalist.'"

DAVID SUZUKI

Going green is another opportunity to create happiness in life and to feel a love beyond ourselves. For too long, we've regarded our planet as separate from ourselves, when in fact we're one. I believe that we all know that the planet is not something to take from or to conquer or to take for granted. Yet despite knowing this, we live day to day like we're entitled to use and abuse the Earth's resources.

Living a green lifestyle is symbolic of being in touch with how simplicity brings true happiness and how care and contribution brings true love. When we love our planet, which is us, we love ourselves. If we transform the way we interact with nature and our environmental living, and if we get in touch with being conscious, responsible, appreciative, and diligent, chances are pretty good that other areas in our life will be transformed as well.

Shift NOW

As I was writing this chapter, I was staying downtown in a large metropolitan city. Every day, I would walk to my favorite grocery store, with an attached eatery, and sit in the sunroom writing. I would enjoy the beautiful, healthy, in-house made foods and salads, on real dishes with real utensils. As I walked the streets of downtown on my trip there and back, I would see people carrying paper coffee cups, designer purses, plastic bags full of takeout containers, retail shopping bags, bottles of water, etc. People who were eating inside of cafes were eating on Styrofoam plates. People in the malls were talking about a $400 pair of jeans they wanted to buy. People walking down the street were talking about their new chemically dyed hair color. People plugging parking meters were driving big SUVs.

Later, when checking emails and messages in the living room of my girlfriend's place, I watched a video a friend had posted on Facebook regarding the amount of garbage that can be found in open, fresh waters. The video showed flocks of beautiful soaring and nesting birds. Then the video showed image after image of dead bird carcasses, with the birds' stomachs full of plastic bottle caps and other plastic pieces that they had eaten. The carcasses were disintegrating, but the plastic pieces were remaining. I began to wonder: if we only pooled all of the money that people spend on dumping chemicals on their hair to make their hair a different, more desirable color, how much garbage could we clean up from our open waters?

It's time to make some new choices. Be the first domino in a chain reaction or by all means be the second, third, or fourth domino. You might become a leader in a group of people (friends, family, colleagues, etc.), or a follower of some already green folk.

Have you seen Derek Siver's "How to Start a Movement" dancing video on YouTube? Start a movement or join the movement.

Each and every one of us can evaluate our current practices and habits, research information and ideas, and take action. It's time to stop justifying our lack of environmental awareness or action in our daily choices because of the way others live. Let me be the first to say that I'm not perfect and that I'm a wasteful consumer. I have lots of learning to do and changes to make myself. When we get honest about our irresponsibility, it creates a new space to start being responsible.

We each have considerable power in contributing to this green movement—in our own actions and in our ability to influence others' actions. On a personal level, we can all reduce consumption. In our workplaces, we can make suggestions for greener practices. If we own a business, we can take on making a green change. As consumers, we can give feedback to local and corporate companies.

I challenge you to look at all the levels that you can make a green impact in—individual, family and friends, community, city, provincial/state, country, world—and recognize that you have a responsibility to make green choices. I encourage you to consider what's at stake here and make a shift. Each and every one of us committing to taking on a greener lifestyle is more important than anything. Today is the day. Start now.

Get Over Yourself

Some green choices require us to make a commitment to something conceptual. The impact of our ungreen (yes, I made that word up) choices isn't immediately apparent. We don't put the disposable roasting pan in a landfill in our backyard. It's out of sight and out of mind, and we're happy that we saved time on washing dishes. And if I stop using disposable roasting pans and soak, scrub, and rinse a real one, there's no immediate gratification or recognition. I simply need to trust that the time and effort I put in made a difference and was worth it.

We're also making a commitment to something bigger than ourselves. Many of us live like the world of our life is the world. For some people, their world is themselves. For others, their world is themselves and their families. This is a small world to live in. We need to get over ourselves. The world doesn't revolve around us or our families. We are a small speck in the scheme of the world, and we have a big responsibility to treat the world we live in with the same respect that we treat our families with. On a daily basis we need to be respectful, loving, generous, and diligent with our planet.

It's worth reflecting on the correlation of how we relate to the environment and how we relate to life. T. Harv Eker says, "How you do anything is how you do everything." What is the correlation between the way you take care of the Earth and the way you live your life? If you aren't willing to do what it takes for the environment because you're being too lazy, selfish, or ignorant, what does this say about your willingness to do what it takes to create love in your family, to generate results in your work, or to contribute to creating happiness in other people's lives?

As Eker encourages, we need to get honest and consider how we're living in one area of life and how that may be similar to how we're living in other areas of life. For example, are you dumping chemicals into the air by driving a gas-guzzling vehicle, dumping chemicals into your body by drinking Pepsi, and dumping negativity into your relationships by gossiping? If you are too lazy to recycle, are you also too lazy to volunteer and to play with your kids? Do you point to the green activities you already do in order to justify not doing more—and in the next breath, point to the things you already do in relationships in order to justify not doing more. If you are avoiding responsibility for caring for the environment, in what ways are you avoiding responsibility for caring for yourself, your relationships, and your contributions to others? In what ways are you taking from, conquering over, or taking for granted the environment—and in what ways are you taking from, conquering over, or taking for granted someone or something in your life? Are you focused on yourself so that environmental conservation is not of interest, and are you focused on yourself in other areas of your life? Look for the correlations. Consider that how you do environmental conservation is how you do things in other areas of life. This may not be a comfortable inquiry, but you may just see something that you've never seen before. Having this insight, and making a change, could transform your life.

Raise Your Awareness

Many of us aren't aware of our habits and their impact because they've become routine. We're numbed by the amount we waste and consume because it has become a way of life in our culture. When I walk into retail stores, especially large ones, I am astounded with the products that line the walls and shelves from floor to ceiling. What makes me sick to my stomach is imagining dumping all of the product from that store into the landfill, because that's where it's going to end up. What makes me even sicker is thinking about dumping all of the product from all the stores around the world into landfills.

Since activists haven't yet been successful in waking us up, let's wake ourselves up. Our level of awareness needs a boost. We need to shake ourselves up since we're still walking around numb to the impact of our choices. Yes, I'm saying that it's time for us to take responsibility for ourselves! Are you ready to take this on?

Do an experiment. For one week, keep the containers of any beverages you purchase. When you buy a coffee, drink it, and keep the paper cup. Do the same with any pop bottles, juice boxes, etc., that you buy and consume. Collect these in your office, your home, your vehicle. At the end of the week, pool your containers, and evaluate the size of your pile. If you want to take on a bigger and more thrilling game, save all of your containers for a month. Now when you evaluate the size of the mountain that you've accumulated, remember that these are just the disposable beverage containers that are a result of your choices, not any other disposable byproducts of your lifestyle. And remember that this was just for one week, and you are just one person on this planet!

Take on some other actions to raise your awareness around consumption and environmental impact. Go camping to remind yourself of what we really need to get through a day and be happy. Take a trip to the local dump. Watch some videos online that educate on environmental impact. Go check out a slaughter house. Read an article on the environmental impacts of travel. Go on a juice diet for three days. Tour a water treatment plant. Research the environmental impacts of the business practices in the industry you work in. Volunteer at a Salvation Army, thrift store, or the like. Visit the dirtiest and most polluted areas where you live or vacation. Push yourself to get out of your bubble.

Because we fail to see how products are produced, packaged, transported, and then disposed of, we're grossly disconnected from the true impacts of our everyday choices. Our day-to-day necessities and luxuries are at our fingertips so long as we have the money to buy them. We fail to appreciate the energy and cost that goes into ensuring that we have clean water flowing through our taps. So long as we pay our water bill (or the landlord does), we subconsciously think that we have a right to clean water. We rarely consider the raw materials used for an item, and the resources needed to produce and deliver the item to us in the marketplace. Our main questions are: 1) Do I want it? and 2) Do I have the money for it? We take for granted what we use and ignore what we waste. If our backyards were to become our own personal landfill, our awareness of our own wasteful choices would heighten very quickly.

Be Educated

One of the biggest challenges in living greener is to have the information that's actually going to make the difference. Paper or plastic? Online shopping or bricks-and-mortar shopping? Gas or diesel? It's fine to want to do the right thing and to make green choices, but we need to know what the facts are in order to make a positive difference.

In the age where online information is at our fingertips, we're in a perfect position to be educated. All it takes is some time and interest to get educated about green choices. Rather than simply following the crowd, we can put some thought and diligence behind our daily choices. It's easy to justify continuing to do what you have always done, even when you suspect that it's not the green things to do—especially when everyone else is doing it. People used to burn Styrofoam in campfires. Some people still buy and wear fur coats and pour solvents down the drain. Today fewer people do these things. We all know that what seems normal and okay in a society in one age can change in the next age, yet when we're living in the current age, we often fail to think critically. We just follow the crowd and/or the norms of yesterday.

Did you know that there are toxins in the ink printed on receipts, which gets onto our hands, into our food, into our water, and into recycled products? Did you know that global consumption of bottled water continues to go up, even though it takes three times the same amount of water—and one-quarter of the amount of oil—to produce one bottle of water? Did you know that species of fish are diminishing rapidly because of overfishing and warmer ocean temperatures? Did you know that it takes in the range of 10,000 liters of water to produce one pair of jeans?

What are 10 things that you will seek more information on?

1. _____

2. _____

3. _____

4. _____

5. _____

6. _____

7. _____

8. _____

9. _____

10. _____

Even though we're so removed from how our food and products are produced in our society, we can get connected by seeking information. We don't see the chemicals being used, the water being wasted, the animals being killed, the forests being flattened. We're not out in nature to see the plastic bottle caps in the stomachs of dead birds. We can, however, pull up zillions of articles, videos, blogs, etc., to get educated on environmental impacts and get connected to the real reasons why it's necessary to be making a shift in our daily choices.

Some people say that it's difficult to find good, accurate information because research studies can be skewed or even influenced by political or economic agendas, but I don't think this is a valid reason to remain ignorant and to continue making ungreen choices that degrade the environment. Rather than being apathetic and critical that good information is hard to come by, let's wake up and start opening our eyes to the wealth of information that's out there.

It's probably not a prudent approach to wait for government to pass laws to protect the environment in order to save us from ourselves. We can already see by looking around at the growing environmental devastation that our governments aren't necessarily going to be the force that makes the difference that's now needed. Certainly governments are making efforts. And, if we're waiting for government to educate us and/or to become educated so that government can protect us, we're going to be waiting a long time.

Give It Up

To go green, you may have to give something up. You may need to carry a reusable mug with you instead of taking a disposable one. You may need to have only one or two pairs of jeans instead of eight. You may need to pick up a piece of garbage and put it in the trash instead of walking by. You may need to pay one dollar more for environmentally friendly toilet paper. You may need to walk 20 minutes instead of driving. You may need to carry the pizza box home for recycling instead of throwing it in the trash. You may need to eat more veggies instead of meat. You may need to write a feedback letter to a company instead of ignoring ungreen business practices. You may need to plant a few vegetables in your backyard instead of buying annuals. You may need to wait until the dishwasher is full instead of running it partly empty. Going green may not seem like it will be easy, but some of these things could actually be easy if you let them be. And some of these things could actually make life easier. Anything can become a new normal.

I purchased a high-quality chamois to use for hand-washing my car instead of going to the wand wash bay. What am I giving up? I'm giving up the convenience of having my car cleaned in two to three minutes at the wash bay. But I think the better question is what am I gaining? Since I'm saving the $2–$4 to use the wand wash, I pay my six-year-old son this money to wash the car. He's more than happy to work for the money. We save water by using one small two-liter bucket of water to wash the car rather than liters and liters of water at the wand wash bay. My son is learning about the importance of living green and the value of payment for good work. We're having fun—and learning—with just a little bit of creativity. I'd rather he wash the car than play video games.

Let's give up our justifications for not making green choices because other people don't make green choices. Just because other people do things doesn't make it safe or okay (green) to do them. If we focus on how normal our ungreen choices are, because we look at the ungreen choices others make, nothing is going to change. Justifying bad behavior because we're surrounded by bad behavior is a bad idea.

Many of us justify not giving something up by pointing to what we're already giving up. In other words, we fail to go greener because we focus on how we're already green. If we point to the actions we already do in order to justify the ones that we don't do, nothing is going to change. Maybe you drive a compact car, but you take long, hot showers. Maybe you don't use sandwich bags, aluminum foil, and saran wrap, but you crank the thermostat in the winter while leaving your windows open to the frosty air. Maybe you shop for second hand clothing, but you have a daily newspaper subscription. Whatever your flavor is, take a good look. Commit to being even greener. Just like there's no end to the love we can give in relationships, there's no end to how green we can go in our lifestyle.

Finally, we need to give up the fear of looking bad. Some people don't make green choices because they're so focused on what everyone else is doing (living ungreen) and what these ungreen folk may think of people who choose to live green. They don't want to look weird or uptight for doing something different. But the fact is you can find the confidence to do it anyway. If people are going to judge you because of your commitment to being green, I think there's merit in reconsidering the value you place on their opinion.

I used to think my aunt was weird for always carrying a reusable shopping bag, cursing aluminum foil, composting, and using organic dish soap, among other choices. Now I think she's one of the coolest people I know, especially because she had the guts and confidence to take a stand for a green lifestyle way, way before going green was a familiar conversation.

Reduce

By now, it's commonplace to know that the order of preference in reducing environmental impact is to reduce, reuse, and recycle. Some people consume and then justify their consumption because the item is recyclable. Do you do this? For example, do you take a plastic bag because it's convenient and justify that it's okay because you can recycle the bag? It takes energy to produce the bag, get the used bag to a recycling plant, recycle the materials, and then convert those materials (whatever has been recovered) into a new product. It's a heck of a lot more efficient to just not use the product to begin with. The first place to make changes on a daily basis is to reduce.

In the kitchen, there are endless materials that are convenience related that we can substantially reduce our use of. We use paper towels to clean up a mess, use plastic bags to pack our kids' lunches, use plastic wrap or aluminum foil to cover food in the fridge, use individually wrapped dishwasher tabs, use straws for drinks, use aluminum pans for cooking, use disposable dishes when we have company, etc. To change some of these practices may require some thought and effort, especially if using these items has become a habitual way of life. It's so much easier to throw away an aluminum roasting pan than soak, scrub, and rinse a real one—especially when it seems that there's no payoff or reward for soaking, scrubbing, and rinsing.

Simply reducing the amount of product we use on a daily basis is easy. Imagine if everyone used 50 percent less toothpaste and squeezed an extra five milliliters of toothpaste from the tube. Given the millions of people in the world who use toothpaste every day, and the number of toothpaste tubes that go to the landfill, imagine how much less toothpaste and how many less toothpaste tubes we would consume. The marketing efforts of toothpaste companies have been extremely effective as they continue to show us images of a plump swirl of toothpaste on the toothbrush. This plump swirl represents far more toothpaste than what is actually needed to get the job done. The end result is that companies sell more toothpaste, which, of course, impacts the environment.

There are certain products that we simply need to drastically reduce our consumption of or avoid using all together. Personal and baby wipes are full of chemicals and take ages to disintegrate, even when the packaging says the wipes are flushable. (In fact, wipes are clogging sewer systems and costing taxpayers hundreds of millions of dollars.) When my kids were babies, we used small baby wash cloths for wiping. Disposable diapers are another daily product in many homes. Even though we know they're not a green choice, people continue to use them. When my second child was a baby, she was trained to go in the toilet at one month old. (I highly recommend reading Ingrid Bauer's book *Diaper Free: The Gentle Wisdom of Natural Infant Hygiene*.) When I did buy diapers, usually for nighttime wear, I bought the environmentally friendly ones. On sale, they were the same price as the regular kind.

Cleaning products are comprised of chemicals. Just because items are sold on the market and available doesn't mean that they're healthy and that we should buy them. I had no idea the impact of cleaning products on the environment and on our health in our home. Many people have grown up in homes where cleaning sprays, foams, gels, etc., were used. This is the norm. The chemical smell in the air now produces a psychological reaction that indicates to people that things are clean.

A few years ago, I began using an environmentally friendly line of cleaning products called Norwex. (If you haven't heard of it, I recommend requesting a consultant to come to your house to do a demonstration and invite your friends over. You may do your friends a favor by increasing their lifespan by a few years.) I started using the Norwex window and glass cleaning cloths and was astounded that the cloths cleaned far better with just water than any chemical I had ever used. As I used more and more Norwex products, the more I was astounded with how well they worked.

We can also reduce by avoiding buying and using products that are designed to be disposable. For instance, I have a razor that I just change the blades on rather than throwing out the entire razor on a regular basis. I have a lint brush that works like magic, and it is not the type that you peel off stickers and put them in the garbage. I bought a Keurig coffee machine only when I discovered that I could buy the refillable coffee baskets rather than the throw away pods. Products that are designed to be thrown out and repurchased are the worst products to buy.

Avoiding buying too much and wasting is another great reduce strategy. I've had friends living with roommates say that they could fully feed themselves on all of the food that their roommates throw out. I used to buy and waste so much food. I would go to the grocery store, buy excessive amounts of food, and then throw out a bunch of the food a week later. Our pantry at home now holds about one-third less of the food that it used to. Packing up and moving homes five times in a period of two years helped me to realize how needless it is to have excessive food on hand.

I used to buy a lot of clothing, especially when it was on sale and I thought I may wear it at some point. A girlfriend of mine woke me up one day when she said, "I only buy things that I LOVE. It doesn't matter if it's on sale. I need to LOVE it." It was also a wakeup call for me to read a number of articles reporting that second-hand clothing stores are overwhelmed with clothing. I had always thought that if I didn't wear something, it would be passed to someone else and go to good use. The better answer is to buy way less. The number of articles of clothing that we actually need is far less than what most of us have.

Rather than keeping unused items around the house, make sure you return them to the store. How many unused items do you have lying around your home? I either tape my receipt to purchases or put the receipt in an envelope that holds all of the receipts for the purchases I have made that month. I generally keep the monthly envelopes for a year. This allows me to find the receipt if I later decide that we don't need the item or it's not suitable. There have been times when one store declined returning an item, and I proceeded to the next store location to return the item.

Focus on buying items that can be returned for a refund and that have longer return periods. If you only have a short amount of time to return the item, the return date may pass before you can choose whether you really use the item or if it really works for you. If you only receive a store credit when you return the item, you're still committed to purchasing a product from that store at some point.

Making a change isn't necessarily easy. Most of us are on a path to live and consume in a certain way and to consume more and more every day. We're attracted to things that are convenient, and we're surrounded by marketing that wants to convince us that we'll be happier when products make our lives easier. So when making a shift to reduce consumption, there may be choices you need to make that require a little more effort. Rather than throwing an individually wrapped pack of two cookies into your child's lunch, put two cookies into a reusable container. Rather than buying a bottle of water, wait until you get to a water fountain or get home to have a drink of water. Rather than leaving your vehicle running, shut it off. (Many environmental groups say that if you're going to idle for more than 10 seconds, you should turn off your engine—unless you're in street traffic, of course.)

In reducing and moving to a greener lifestyle, it's time to get our minds out of the gutter and try something new. At first I was horrified that a small tub of cleaning paste would cost over $30 from Norwex. But a year later, the jar is still two-thirds full and it's the best cleaning product that I've ever purchased. The paste safely and effectively cleans the scratches and rust on my car, my kitchen sinks, the grout of my tile, etc. After years of believing that Comet spray was the only cleaner that would actually clean my shower, I replaced the toxic Comet bottle in my home with a Norwex cleaner, which is safe and tough on scum. I can breathe easy while I'm using it knowing that I'm not spraying chemicals into the air that will kill me and my children—and the environment.

Don't assume that making changes is going to be hard. Sometimes it's not actually a choice that takes more time or money, but just a different, conscious choice. You may choose to enjoy your drink without a straw, or only take one paper napkin rather than a handful. It takes the same amount of time to place a sandwich for a packed lunch in a container as it does a sandwich bag. It's time to get out of habits and patterns.

Make Daily Choices

We can try to trick ourselves into thinking that our footprint doesn't really make a difference in the environment, but the truth is that it does. Imagine what a different world we would live in if everyone walked around every day thinking about how they could minimize their environmental impact instead of thinking about how they can have more and do more. Imagine if everyone made conscious choices instead of living on autopilot.

I propose that there is another R we can add to the 3R equation: reflect. We can reduce, reflect, reuse, and recycle. If we're not able to reduce consumption or avoid consumption completely, then we can reflect on what we're buying. In order to reflect and make conscious decisions, this can require information and education, as we were discussing earlier.

Companies have started showing us on their packaging how they contribute to reducing environmental impact. For instance, on a box of water, a company states the following:

- 76 percent of the box is composed of a renewable resource: trees;

- The trees come from well-managed FSC-certified forests;

- The company ships its boxes flat to a filler to lower its carbon footprint;

- The boxes are recyclable at participating facilities; and

- The company donates to reforestation and world water relief efforts.

If there is an actual need to buy a container of water, when given a choice between this box of water and a bottle of water, it would make sense after reflecting to buy the box of water. Whether we're buying envelopes, coffee, chocolate, yard waste bags, or anything, we can become more aware of what has gone into the product so that we can make greener choices.

In any buying decision, we can reflect on what product will stand the test of time so that it may be used and loved for years or reused. Rather than buying the $12 pair of rubber boots for my kids, which have fallen apart by end of season in past, I chose to buy a $40 pair of boots ($50 regular price but on sale for $40) so that they could be reused rather than thrown in the garbage. I will be able to sell the boots again for $20–$25, so there's little difference to my pocket book.

I buy clothing that stands the test of time and reduces our family's footprint. Peekaboo Beans children's playwear is a high-quality brand of clothing that's designed for kids' comfort and independence. Fast fashion is designed for kids to grow out of and wash terribly so that people throw the clothing away and buy new. They end up washing it a few times and the piece looks nothing like it did when it was new on the rack. Peekaboo Beans is designed to last. The company has designed "grow with me" pieces that can last children two to three years. Because of the style and design, a dress becomes a tunic, and the tunic becomes a shirt. The quality of the fabric is high so the pieces still look like new wash after wash. The clothing is also created to mix and match; rather than buying clothing in outfits, you can buy a few tops and bottoms to mix and match them all. You end up buying fewer pieces, and even though they're worn more, they usually last longer than clothing sold through retail chains. And finally, people sell their used Peekaboo Beans playwear via Facebook fan pages to other people who appreciate the quality, comfort, and style of the brand. Parents recuperate a good chunk of the money they spent on the clothing and prevent the clothes from going to the landfill.

After we've endeavored to reduce and reuse, we can look at recycling. There are many people who throw items away such as bottles, cans, paper, cardboard, etc., either on a regular basis or sporadically because it's easier. In our home, we have three tall, narrow bins under the sink that hold bottles and cans, garbage, and mixed recyclable items (glass, paper, cardboard, etc.). We're fortunate that our municipal recycling program allows for all mixed recyclable items to be placed in one recyclable bag; otherwise, we would have additional bins under the sink or in another place.

People in my life bug me about carrying around garbage in my hands, purse, suitcase, and car, but I'm happy to do it if it means that I can get an item to a recycle bin rather than it being thrown away. In leaving from a stay at a girlfriend's condo, I was rolling a suitcase and carrying a large duffel bag over my shoulder. I was holding a large, empty, and clean plastic salad tub in my hand to take down to her recycling area as I left. (She's not an avid recycler. I often dig clean recyclable cardboard out of her garbage while staying with her. So I wasn't convinced that she would recycle the large, plastic salad tub if I didn't.) However, I realized that I had left my girlfriend's key tag with her, which I needed in order to access the downstairs garbage disposal and recycling area. No, I didn't throw the plastic salad tub in the garbage. I promptly flattened the tub, slipped it in my suitcase, and off I went to carry the plastic tub home to recycle.

There's certainly no shortage of ideas on how to make small daily choices and even lifestyle changes to reduce your environmental impact. The point of this chapter is not to bring forward the particular ideas, but to prompt you to take on a host of new ideas on your own. There's a lot more power in making the conscious, personal decision to take on some new practices than being told to do something. You know you best. What are you actually willing to take on?

What are some daily choices that you're committed to make?

_____

_____

_____

_____

_____

_____

_____

Create a Green Day

Some of us have a fear of commitment when it comes to making green choices, especially if we think that it's going to interfere with our lifestyle. I'm absolutely advocating that we stop being ignorant and selfish and seriously look at shifting our lifestyle for the sake of our planet. But if you need to ease into this shift of being greener and to take some baby steps without full commitment, how about creating a green day to try out a few new things?

Spend one day fully taking on the lens of how you can reduce your environmental impact in every action you take and choice you make. You might surprise yourself. This might even be fun. You may even decide to share this new game with friends who decide they fancy it. Heaven knows, this could become trendy.

Although there are oodles and oodles of green ideas that are simple and effective, here are some ideas to spark your thoughts:

- Request that your bills and statements be emailed/paperless.

- If it's yellow, let it mellow.

- Turn down the heat two degrees, or turn up the air conditioning two degrees.

- Decline having your flowers wrapped when you buy them.

- Fold and put away your clothes to wear again rather than automatically throwing them in the laundry.

- Go to a local farmer's market.

- Walk instead of drive.

- When asking for a glass of water at a coffee shop, request that it be in a washable porcelain mug instead of a to-go disposable plastic cup.

- Use matches instead of lighters.

- Opt out of using plastic utensils if you can do without them.

- Post something green related on Facebook.

- Buy items only if you can return them so you're not stuck with them if you talk yourself into not needing them.

- Turn the lights and electronics off in your home.

- Call a company and request that you be taken off of their paper mailing list.

• Carry a water bottle with you.

• Decline accepting or taking a handful of napkins. When there are extras, take them home with you to use instead of Kleenex or paper towel.

• Borrow a book from the library or download an electronic version, instead of buying a paper copy.

• Pick the smaller bag when you're buying bulk foods.

• When printing something, print on the clean side of an already printed sheet of paper.

• Buy someone a consumable gift, especially if you were planning to buy something useless.

• Rather than gossiping with friends, chat about green products and green solutions.

• Wrap the restaurant food you would like to take home with you in the napkin that is on the table rather than requesting a takeout container (this works better for some foods).

• Walk around your house looking for products you can return to the store and then return them.

• Send a feedback email to a business about how they could implement a greener practice.

There are a million things you can do. Books have been written. Buy an e-book or borrow a book from the library.

Are you thinking that these are little things? Or that you don't have time? Or that you can't be bothered? These are all excuses. Take a moment to get present to the excessive consumption in our society, and the serious degradation of our environment. Let it sink in and allow yourself to acknowledge the state of emergency that we're in. If you saw a child walking onto the road with cars whizzing past only a few feet ahead, would you say that it's just a little thing, or that you don't have time, or that you can't be bothered to do anything about it? No, you would save the child. Do the same for our planet. Do what needs to be done.

Take a Stand

This is where you can start making an impact at a level beyond yourself. And this is what's going to make a real difference in people's health and happiness on this planet in the long run. Are you up to make a real difference?

It isn't someone else's job to take a stand. We all know that we make a direct impact with our choices and also inspire others. Taking a stand may mean taking a few more minutes, writing a letter, or paying a few extra dollars, but you can take a strong stand for the environment. Look for ways to take a stand in your daily routine, in a project you get involved in, in the people you influence, or otherwise.

As I go about my day, I'm more than happy to take a little bit more time and effort, or even create a little bit of upset, to demonstrate my stand for reducing environmental impact. One example of something I take a stand on is bags. You will often see me and the kids carrying a few items or even an armload of items out of a grocery store or retail store without a bag. There have been times when I've had to be very firm with the clerk, saying that I don't want a bag. Sometimes I'll say to the clerk that I don't need a bag and the clerk will put the items in a bag anyway. I'll say again, "Thank you, I don't need a bag." There have been times when it has seemed that the clerk is upset that I don't want a bag.

They have tried to give me a bag even after I have declined two or more times. I sometimes remove the items from the bag myself. Because I've learned that clerks may then throw the bag in the garbage rather than use it with the next customer, I'll now re-hang the plastic bag on the bag rack or fold the paper bag back down to ensure the clerk uses it for the next purchase. I don't worry about people thinking I'm crazy because I think they're crazy to not care. When going through certain drive-thrus (hey, I admitted that I'm not perfect), I've learned that I need to say at the time of ordering that I don't want a bag with my order. Otherwise, if I drive through, then they'll have automatically put my order in a bag out of procedure. In coffee shops, as I'm ordering my pastry at the cash register, I state that I don't need my item in a bag. If a different employee is responsible for retrieving my pastry and hasn't heard my request, I catch her/his attention and state again, "I don't need a bag, thank you."

When out with my girlfriend, author Sandra Gangel, at an eatery, she noticed that the business's practice was to staple the cash register receipt to the credit card receipt. Sandra took two minutes to inform the cashier of the incredible waste that staples create in our society. For a moment, I thought she was crazy and fussing over small things, but then my judgement of her was replaced by a deeper respect for her. Sandra was willing to take the time, risk judgment, and speak out to educate and take a stand. She was a new friend at the time, who has now become a close friend who I admire in many ways. These are the kinds of friends I want in my life.

When other people see us taking a stand, we're contributing to a perception that green choices and taking a stand for the environment is normal. We're moving closer to the tipping point of people living green and making green choices. Just by observing us, people will start to see that they could go greener, too. It's an indirect impact.

Taking a stand can also look like striving to impact directly and to speak up. I wrote a feedback email to a large coffee chain to express my concern that they were putting recyclable four-liter milk jugs in the garbage. I also expressed my concern that sometimes when I take in my reusable coffee mug, I've seen the staff measuring the correct amount of coffee in a paper cup, dumping it in my reusable mug and then throwing the paper cup away—which, of course, entirely defeats the purpose of me bringing in a reusable mug. I have no problem taking three minutes to send a quick note to a company knowing that my comments could save heaps of plastic and paper from going to the landfill.

Sometimes it takes courage to speak up, but do it anyway. Encourage your child's school, sports team, or hobby group to sell a consumable item for a fundraiser rather than a product that will eventually end up in the landfill. I'm always excited to see groups selling items like gift cards for grocery stores for fundraisers. A girlfriend of mine and her husband own a honey-producing company. They produce raw honey straight from the hive. I encouraged this girlfriend to create a fundraising program through their company so that groups can offer a quality, consumable product in their fundraising programs.

If you see someone making an ungreen choice, say something. What may seem like a little thing that people do can add up to big things that we all do. For instance, imagine someone you know is about to use a white hotel towel to clean up a dirty mess. It may seem harmless, right? The towel is handy and it's not yours, right? But the hotel needs to use strong chemicals to get it clean or dispose of the towel (and replace it) if it's ruined. Simply ask this person to hold up and help her or him to find something more suitable to clean up the mess. That's it. That's all.

Taking a stand can also look like joining a group that has a stand. There are many worthwhile local, national, and international projects to get involved with in order to contribute to making a difference. When people come together in groups, the level of the difference that can be made is multiplied. A friend of mine is involved in a project that has been created in India to plant 10 million trees. Another friend of mine has created a game that allows people to explore how they can create a greener lifestyle (http://www.omega.verdigo.com/). At the end of the day, there are endless opportunities for getting involved if we open our eyes to them.

Real changes are made when people take a stand, take action, and speak up. Changes are starting to be made. Some municipalities are banning the sale of bottles of water; some stores are charging consumers for plastic bags; some stores require their cashiers to ask customers if they want a receipt; some bank machines now accept deposits without envelopes. New norms are emerging. These are all steps forward and they've happened because a number of people took a stand.

Step Over Challenges

"To be a champion, I think you have to see the big picture. It's not about winning and losing; it's about everyday hard work and about thriving on a challenge. It's about embracing the pain that you'll experience at the end of a race and not being afraid. I think people think too hard and get afraid of a certain challenge."

SUMMER SANDERS

The fact is that life is full of challenges, obstacles, and bumps in the road. We all know this. This is not a revolutionary concept. In fact, this is the design and purpose of life. We need to taste the sour to taste the sweet. To expect anything different is to have your head in the clouds.

If you're stopped by a challenge in one area of your life, chances are that a similar challenge is holding you back in other areas of life. Again, "How you do anything is how you do everything." This is the purpose of the coaching work I do with my clients—exploring the barriers that are holding people back in an area of life, and breaking through them to create breakthroughs in all areas of life.

When we stress about challenges, we're not being chill for ourselves or the people around us. Nobody likes to be around someone who's being whiney, fearful, lazy, or a victim. I would guess if you get real honest with yourself, you don't even like to be around yourself when you're being any of these.

Stepping over challenges is a mindset and a practice. An openness and a willingness to self-reflect are required to step over challenges, in addition to some real courage and commitment. People who step over challenges aren't born a different way. They choose to live a different way rather than being ruled by the human condition. In the human condition, there's doubt and fear and excuses. A commitment to being extraordinary, and contributing on an extraordinary level, defies the human condition. No matter the challenge, you can step over it. In fact, you can leap over it with flying colors if you choose to.

Keep Things in Perspective

When we put things into perspective, many of the things that we perceive as challenges are not really challenges. People sit in coffee shops complaining about how their pants don't fit right, or how their mother calls them too much, or how the price of gas has gone up when there are children in the community who are going to school without eating breakfast. People sit at work counting down the number of days remaining before they can retire and gossiping about who's sleeping with whom when there are women working as sexual slaves all over the world. People walk through the store trying to figure out what to buy someone as a gift and worry about how much to spend and whether they'll like it when the landfills are full of garbage.

I think it's time for a number of us to do a reality check on whether our challenges are actually challenges. With all the time and energy we waste on little things, we could be up to taking on big things. Rather than running around town to find the freshest tomatoes and perfect place settings for a dinner party, how about donating money to the food bank or volunteering at a soup kitchen? Believe me, your dinner party guests won't notice the difference in the taste of the tomatoes and probably won't know if you purchased new napkins, but the people who don't have the means to eat at all will sure appreciate a meal. Let's get out of our little bubbles and remind ourselves of what a challenge really is.

In getting ready to go on a two-week vacation in December, it occurred to me that it would make economic sense to rent out my home for the time we would be away rather than pay someone to shovel the snow off the sidewalks. After making the decision to rent the house, every day I put the thought into the universe that I was ready for the perfect renter to come along and enjoy being in our home. In addition to putting my clear and powerful request into the universe, I took action. I mentioned to some friends that my home would be available in case they heard of anyone looking for a place to stay. I also posted an online advertisement in two places.

Sure enough, the perfect renter came along. I received an email asking if our home was available. I replied and said that it was available for two weeks in December while we would be on vacation. The respondent stated that they needed a place for the entire month. I called my mom to ask if we could stay with her for one week prior to our vacation and one week after our vacation. My mom was incredibly generous and gracious and agreed.

In the following days as the renter and I exchanged emails to set up our arrangement, I found out that his wife was scheduled for two neurosurgeries in the coming month to remove cancer.

The couple had a two-month-old baby. It would be the husband, the wife's parents, the husband's parents, and the baby staying in our home when they weren't at the hospital. Despite the situation, the renter's email was factual and succinct. My stomach turned and my eyes welled with tears as I read the email. My heart and body was instantly filled with gratitude for my life. I could not imagine what it would be like to be in the situation they were in. What seemed like challenges in my life paled in comparison. It was the very least we could do to vacate our home for a month so that this family had a warm home to envelope them for a month and over the upcoming holiday season.

We all experience challenges. While our own challenges are usually overwhelming for us, we need to remember that others are often dealing with bigger challenges down the block, across the city, throughout the country, and around the world. Remembering that there are bigger problems in the world keeps us grounded. We can chill out when what we think is a big problem shifts to become a small problem.

Define Who You're Committed to Be

There seems to be a prevailing notion that extraordinary people were born that way, even though we know it's not true. We trick ourselves into thinking that those who "make it" are special. We know that behind success is hard work and perseverance, but we let ourselves off the hook from stepping up to challenges and generating accomplishment. We tell ourselves things like, "That's just not me," or "I don't have what it takes," or "It's not the right time," because we're afraid of challenges or even afraid of success.

Here are two questions to answer:

1. Who do I want to be?

_____

_____

_____

_____

2. Who am I committed to be?

_____

_____

_____

_____

_____

_____

These are two very different questions. Write down your immediate response to the first question. I encourage you to continue reflecting on both questions at a deeper level.

Often the first question is related to our feelings of what we think we want, which can be dictated by ego and a desire to look good. We want to impress our friends and family, and to be accepted and approved of in the context of the culture we live in. We want praise, and we want to fit in. It's a good idea to question your first, quick responses to the question of who you want to be. Really look at the reasons behind why you want to be somebody. You may think you want to be somebody, but it may not even be realistic because it contradicts your own values and priorities.

One of the most common pitfalls of wanting to be someone is that people are trying to impress someone else or be better for the sake of other people's regard, approval, or a reward. We have a picture or a story—a fantasy—of this someone that we think we should or could be. A common source of the fantasy is who we think our parents want us to be. Many people are still subconsciously wanting to be someone for their parents and trying to prove something to their parents, even years after they've left their parents' home and sometimes years after their parents have passed. Consider the extent to which you're striving to impress your parents, friends, colleagues, or anyone else for the sake of praise, affinity, money, or some other reason.

Who you're committed to be is a deeper and more powerful question. It's who you intend to be regardless of your own doubts, your circumstances, and the challenges you encounter. It's who you're committed to be regardless of what other people are doing and what you think they want you to be. You'll run, jump, swim, and fly to be this person. You'll dig deep to develop yourself to be this person. You'll feel in your heart and gut the difference you'll make in this world in being this person. The motivating force needs to be for yourself and/or to contribute to others. This is authentic. Anything else is inauthentic.

Almost all people we consider to be extraordinary—academics, artists, politicians, philanthropists, inventors, etc.—say that they're simply ordinary people. This is very true. They drink water, eat food, sleep, and have sex. They're ordinary people who put one foot in front of the other, take action, and continue to step over little and big challenges on a day-to-day basis. As the accomplishments become greater, the challenges often do as well. This is just how it works. They coordinate their families and teams of staff members. They donate to local charities and create charity events and organizations. They support their circles of friends and faithfully mentor many budding professionals. The game is bigger. Inevitably, so are the challenges.

It's essential to create a powerful driving force behind what you're setting out to accomplish in order to have the wherewithal to step over challenges. Setting a goal won't necessarily work. It's essential to be in touch with the why behind the goal and what you're setting out to accomplish. The why is what will push you through the mundane, emotional, time-consuming, physically demanding hurdles. The key behind the goal is the reason why you want to achieve it. If you're working to achieve the goal just for the goal, there's going to be far less power behind it.

In dating, I have an intention to create a partnership. One why for me is so that my children can experience family, love, and connection as they continue to grow. It's extremely important to me that they see what a healthy partnership looks like in terms of unconditional love, communication, quality time, support, and conflict resolution. For my daughter, I've committed to make sure she sees how a smart, motivated, independent woman can also choose to be loving, gracious, and dependent. For my son, I've committed to make sure he sees and feels a male presence and learns what it takes to be a strong, successful man who can be powerful with any kind of person, and who can communicate both directly and empathically. This why creates real importance and even time pressure in creating a partner in life and love. All of a sudden my nervousness toward meeting new people, my nervousness to get dressed up and go out with a stranger, and my self-consciousness of dating as a single mom seem like challenges that I can overcome. No longer is dating about me avoiding becoming an old, lonely lady because of my own fear and ego. There is something bigger and deeper at stake and there is urgency to it.

In writing this book, the why for me is to make a difference on this planet by empowering people to be happy and loving, thus raising the vibration in this world. My intention is to make a difference for people who wonder if there may be more to life. Some people believe they're happy or okay, and that that's as good as it gets. Others feel lost, like they live in a fog. Both male and female friends share with me that it seems they're "missing something" in life. I'm committed to make sure people unleash the abundant love and energy that is within them so that they can contribute to their families, communities, and the world.

People have asked me over the years how I've made such a shift in my personal and professional life, how I stay motivated to be in action, and how I get so much accomplished. It became clear that people wanted to hear about my experience and my thoughts. Although writing a book has taken many, many, many days and so much energy, it happens to be a very effective way to articulate a number of ideas clearly in one package. Sure, it would've been wonderful to have been drinking a cold drink and sitting on the beach in Mexico, but I was just as happy to sit in the hotel lobby with a cold drink and work on writing this book for a few hours because I knew that it was going to make a difference. Me sitting on the beach for a few hours wasn't going to make a difference. I also would've quite enjoyed watching movies many evenings, but I was content sitting in my bed writing with my laptop knowing that I was on track with sharing my passion and purpose. I'm clear that I'm committed to be someone who makes a difference.

In stepping over a challenge, there are actions to take that we may be fearful of. The actions become much easier to take when we keep in mind the context or bigger picture of what we're up to. When I jumped out of an airplane with a parachute on my back, I didn't have a goal of jumping out of an airplane. I had a strong desire to skydive in order to feel the freedom and exhilaration of free-falling through the air and knowing that I had the courage to take on an extreme activity. The experience of skydiving is what had me overcome the fear of putting the parachute on, getting into the plane, and jumping out the door of the plane.

What would you like to accomplish in different areas of your life? Possible areas Include health, family, finances, friends, partnership (spouse), communication, volunteering, leisure, career, spirituality, community, and sexuality. In the following areas, what are you striving for? What is your why? What do you see as possible challenges?

Area: _____

Striving for: _____

WHY: _____

Possible Challenges: _____

_____

_____

Area: _____

Striving for: _____

WHY: _____

Possible Challenges: _____

_____

_____

Area: _____

Striving for: _____

WHY: _____

Possible Challenges: _____

_____

_____

Area: _____

Striving for: _____

WHY: _____

Possible Challenges: _____

_____

_____

Make Fear a Former Friend

It's not the fear of challenge that gets in the way—it's being paralyzed by the fear that gets in the way. You've probably heard the saying, "Feel the fear and do it anyway." People who get things done aren't necessarily fearless. They take action in the face of fear. When other people are taking the leap and overcoming their fears, it may seem like they don't have any fear. This may be true but probably isn't.

When we avoid challenges—when we're more focused on the obstacle itself and our fear rather than on how to deal with it—it's evident that the challenge will remain. The obstacle isn't likely to get smaller, and it may actually get bigger. For instance, if there's a health challenge to deal with and there's fear about looking silly exercising, the health challenge is likely to grow.

The challenge may get bigger in reality, and it may also get bigger in our mind. As swimming Olympian Summer Sanders points out, when we think too hard, our mind talks us out of things. When we don't "feel the fear and do it anyway," the fear can continue to build and become even more overwhelming. There's always a possibility that our fears will come true, but we usually build them up in our minds. We imagine the worst possible scenarios.

One of the keys to stepping over challenges is not to dwell on them. Dwelling can look like daydreaming about them, journaling about them, getting emotional about them, and talking about them with other people. We often think about what's going to go wrong, how we're not good enough to tackle the challenge, or some other negative thought. Rarely do we daydream about how the obstacle is going to be manageable or how we're going to surpass it with flying colors. When we dwell, we make the challenge bigger in our mind.

In my own life, I've been practicing not feeling fear and not dwelling. When I start to feel fear, I quickly inquire into whether it's a bad gut feeling or me just being fearful—fearful of hard work, fearful of success, fearful of others' judgments, etc. If it's truly a bad gut feeling, then I reconsider moving forward. It's so critical though to distinguish between a bad gut feeling and fear.

If I'm fearful, and if it's not a bad gut feeling, rather than trying to figure out why I'm fearful or justify why I'm fearful, I focus on action steps. I seek coaching, exercise, sleep, or take action to release it. The more I focus on what needs to be done and the mini tasks that are required to get something done, the more I'm focused on putting one foot in front of the other. Rather than thinking about what I don't want to do and why I don't want to do it, I come up with ideas on how I can get things done quickly and easily. Rather than allowing fantasies and emotions to consume my energy, I take action.

If I find that I am still daydreaming about my fears, then it's a sign to me that I must have extra energy to spare. When there's a demanding list of action steps to take, there's little space for daydreaming. There is only a need for action. Daydreaming is fruitless, so if I find myself caught up in fearful daydreaming or dwelling, then I up the ante on a project I'm involved in or take on something new. This creates a more demanding to-do list. I'd rather be advancing my game or creating a bigger game than getting bogged down in dwelling.

After I'd been single for about a year, it was time to start seriously looking at dating. A number of people in my life had suggested that, after separating with a partner, it's beneficial to take a year to recover emotionally and get grounded. So after a year of flying solo, I decided it was time to get out there. I had never in my life been keen on dating, and I was now even less keen to date as a single mom. I had high hopes of a friend setting me up with an awesome guy and us falling in love right away so that I wouldn't even have to explore the dating scene. However, referrals from friends weren't streaming in. A number of people suggested that I try online dating, but I kept holding out for my fantasy of the dream referral relationship to unfold.

On New Year's Day, despite the anxiety and fear, I paid for 365 days of service on an online dating site that many friends had said was professional and offered a legitimate matching system. My fears included seeing my ex online, going on a first date with a stranger, being stood up, having awkward conversation, and being stalked afterward. Maybe my fear was that I wouldn't meet anyone interesting and suitable and end up becoming an old lady with a house full of cats. Any of these possibilities could actually unfold, with some being more likely to take shape in reality than others. (By the way, I didn't see my ex online, but I did see his co-worker online.)

With my fear of being stalked, rather than daydream about my fear, I took action. I took a friend's advice to use a pseudo name when I created my online profile. I used pictures that weren't otherwise posted online to prevent people from using face recognition technology to identify me. And, I reminded myself of my why—my intention to create partnership and family. When I received the first few messages from men who were interested in me, feelings of fun and excitement dissipated many of my various feelings of fear.

Often our minds create a mixed bag of fears, some small and some big, some likely and some highly unlikely. We're faced with fears of things we think, things we hear other people say, and things we see in the media. In other words, sometimes our fears aren't even our own fears—they're ideas that we've taken on as our own.

When faced with a challenge, the first thing to ask is "What am I afraid of?" Sometimes what we're most afraid of is success. When I began dating again, there was a part of me that was fearful to find a match and to fall in love again. Behind that fear of success was a fear that I may experience a breakup and broken heart again, and an even deeper fear that I didn't have the ability to be a good partner.

Fear can become a former friend if that's the choice we make. Sometimes we befriend fear because it enables us to stay stuck. Fear can become an acquaintance in our lives. It's something that's there that we see from time to time. We can carry on with our life in alignment with our intentions and higher purpose, even with fear as an acquaintance. When we face and acknowledge what our fears really are in any given situation, they usually start to look smaller and more manageable. And if the fears still look big, we can still choose to act in spite of them.

Use Powerful Words

On the playground, I heard a mom saying to her son, "Be careful." Then, as she was watching her daughter playing, she said to her daughter, "Be careful." She continued to say "be careful" throughout the time we were at the playground. I wondered how being careful dictates how she lives her life.

When I'm at the playground with my kids, I encourage them to be both mindful and to take risks. When they're going to jump off of something, I say things like, "Okay...just notice how high that is." My intention is to teach them to consider the challenge and to decide for themselves how they're going to handle it. My rule at the playground with my kids has always been that if you need an adult to help you, then you need to figure out how to do it on your own, ask another child for help, or wait until you're big enough to do it on your own. (I believe that an adult helping can create a situation of "saving," while another child helping creates a situation of teamwork.) This has taught them to take risks if they really want to do something. And it has also taught them that they need to tackle things that are within their range of abilities.

It's particularly helpful to develop a vocabulary that supports you in stepping over challenges. These can become your new favorite buzzwords. They'll actually trick your mind into believing that what seems like a challenge is no big deal. They might sound like:

- No problem.

- No worries.

- That's nothing.

- It's all good.

- Easy peasy (lemon squeezy).

- No biggie.

- That's a cake walk.

- I've got this.

- No big deal.

- Let's carry on.

- Easy breezy.

- That's it?

- I can handle that.

- It's taken care of.

- I'm so grateful for what I'm learning.

- Onward and upward.

Pick the words that resonate for you and create your own. Start saying these words in your head and out loud anytime you perceive even the tiniest obstacle. This becomes a habit, which becomes a mindset.

What are your powerful words?

_____

_____

_____

_____

_____

_____

Reach Out

Many of us live life alone without even realizing how we do this or how often we do it. In other words, we have become so independent, solitary, and disconnected as a way of living every day that we don't even realize the extent to which we are doing it.

Reaching out for support requires more courage than not reaching out. It takes guts to admit what we're dealing with and what's stopping us. One thing that I've learned over the years is to let go of trying to be perfect. A mentor of mine, Vik Maraj, said, "Nobody admires someone who's perfect, Kara. People want to know that you're a normal human being, dealing with the same normal things that they are. Everybody out there is trying to look like they have it all together. It's ordinary to want to look put together. It's extraordinary to admit that you don't have it together."

This doesn't mean reaching out to people to complain about and dwell on problems, but rather reaching out to people to request that they help you identify and confront your barriers. Believe me, the people in your life probably don't want to hear you whine or struggle. (And if they do, take a look at your social circle.) They do want to see you happy and experiencing love in your life. They want to see you chill.

I used to think that I had enough friends. In fact, a girlfriend of mine who I met in university still bugs me to this day because when we met, I said to her, "I don't really need any more friends. I have enough." Luckily, she's an exceptional woman, and she pushed through my wall to be a friend of mine. She has made a wonderful difference in my life.

Over time, and especially through the personal and professional development courses I have taken, I looked at what this resistance to having friends was really about. I discovered that I had a deep-seated need to prove that I was okay on my own. I began to see something in my life that I had never seen before. I saw that I wouldn't let people in and that I would push people away. I had built rigid walls around me that prevented me from being deeply and authentically connected to people in all areas of my life.

I decided that it was high time for a shift, so I challenged my own notion of believing that a few good friends in life are plenty. I pushed myself to imagine the possibility of having hundreds or even thousands of friends. I also had to push the boundaries of my own notions of what a friend is and accept that a relationship with a friend doesn't have to look a certain way. People don't have to communicate with me a certain number of times per month, or work in a certain profession, or be a certain age, or help me a certain amount to be considered a friend. Anyone can be a friend for any reason. I've found that with far less expectations of what a friend looks like, I'm now very open to connecting with different people in different ways and forming different kinds of friendships.

I've never had so many incredible relationships and friends in my life to reach out to every day.

Now, in looking at the team of people around me, I see my family, my trainer at the gym, my doctor, my spiritual coach, my assistant, my financial planner, my yard man, my networking peeps, my book coach, my babysitters—the list goes on. I used to think that only rich people had a team of people around them. I've come to the realization that being rich in happiness and love requires creating friendships, reaching out, and opening up to the contributions that other people can offer.

In writing *Chill*, there was a flock of people supporting me to complete the book. Friends sent me messages regularly to ask about progress on the book; I had friends who opened their homes while I wrote; I had family (thanks, Dad) who set me up with a book coach; I had author friends who shared advice on writing and publishing a book; I had friends agree to do interviews and share their stories for the book; I had girlfriends who offered to read over chapters. The list goes on and on.

When we get out of our own way and let other people contribute to us, it's amazing the path that opens up and the difference we can all make together. What I want you to understand is that the family and friends who contributed to completing this book did so not entirely for me—but for you. These people all believe in making a positive difference in your life. They see the importance of an abundance of people in this world being in love with themselves, others, and life.

One of my favorite quotes is "It takes a village to raise a child." We're all children, always. We all need the village around us to continue supporting us in our own growth and development. We're all talented and blessed with special gifts, and we're meant to be connected as human beings in order to share our gifts with each other.

We need to support each other as we make a difference on this planet. No one person can do it alone. Certainly, when people offer help, take it. But we also need to know how to reach out for help. It can be a real challenge to be vulnerable, but if that's what it takes to reach out for support in order to conquer a bigger challenge, why not do it?

Look at what you're out to accomplish in your personal life, in your family, in your community, and in the world. In what areas of life do you think you need to reach out for support in? What kind of support would be beneficial? How will you reach out for this support?

Area: _____

Support: _____

_____

_____

How: _____

Area: _____

Support: _____

_____

_____

How: _____

Area: _____

Support: _____

_____

_____

How: _____

Area: _____

Support: _____

_____

_____

How: _____

Area: _____

Support: _____

_____

_____

How: _____

Rest, Rejuvenate and Rock It

It's so important to emphasize that we need to continue filling our energy tanks to stay positive and motivated. When I was writing this chapter, an old friend and colleague texted me to ask what the kids and I were up to for the weekend. I said that the kids were with their dad. He texted back and said, "What are you doing today then? Taking a break and looking after yourself, I hope. Remember how you would say to me that you cannot help others if you do not take care of yourself first? Besides, you work too damn hard." I shared with him that I was doing exactly that. I was out of town, staying with a girlfriend, relaxing, and writing the book.

One of the greatest blessings in life is that we're granted a new day every 24 hours, with an opportunity to sleep in between. When things start to feel hard and the obstacles too great, a good night's sleep can do wonders. Sometimes a brand new perspective or brand new ideas or brand new circumstances emerge the next day that you would never expect. Something pops into your mind, or you run into the perfect person, or something happens in the perfect way.

What can really bog us down in the midst of challenge are our emotions. Fear, tiredness, worry, anger, resentment, and anxiety cloud our thinking and set us on a path of unreasonable action and/or stark paralysis. This is not to say that we can eradicate emotion in our lives so that it doesn't interfere with our ability to step over challenges. It's not possible. But there's a lot to be said for first focusing on resting and rejuvenating so that we can powerfully deal with these emotions. In this vital state, we force ourselves to think rather than to feel. We can put one foot in front of the other rather than talking about our challenges with ourselves and others.

When we're healthy and rested, we're full of life. Our physical and emotional well-being is strong. Even when faced with a challenge, there's less emotional reaction and drama, there are more ideas for actions to take, and there's more energy to take on the next action.

Be honest with yourself and take time to answer the following questions:

When in your life did you have the most physical and emotional vitality? What did you accomplish? How did it feel?

_____

_____

_____

_____

How is your current physical and emotional well-being getting in the way of you stepping over challenges?

_____

_____

_____

_____

What are you committed to shift in your well-being? Why?

_____

_____

_____

_____

See the Gift

One of the most important but hardest things to do is to look at challenges as a gift. To truly believe that challenges happen for a reason and that everything happens in perfect time is a practice and an art. To be okay with exactly how things are, and exactly how things aren't, is to accept a situation for exactly what it is rather than to wish that the challenges didn't exist.

Have you ever looked back on life and realized that something that happened, which was upsetting or difficult at the time, was actually a blessing? Or that a challenge you overcame made you the person you are and set you up powerfully to take something on in life? We can practice being able to see the gift of a challenge in the moment or at least trusting that there is a gift that we aren't yet aware of.

As I was in the depths of pain, anger and loneliness during my divorce—in addition to dealing with some legal complexities and stresses—I had a sense that the experience was happening for a reason. With a good chunk of the population having experienced separation and divorce, I could see that going through this turmoil would certainly help me to relate to the challenges a good number of people have faced in their lives. Separation and divorce is one of the most difficult experiences to move through in life. Given that I'm committed to making a difference in empowering people, this was to become a powerful learning experience in who I'm committed to be.

I now see that my relationship with my ex-husband was a blessing. The strength and wisdom I gained from dealing with his constant criticism, the divorce process, and learning to co-parent together has given me more learning than I could ever ask for— truly. It's been a learning experience in becoming very clear about who I am and what I stand for. I had a taste of the challenge that some people experience in their relationships. I experienced how important it is for people to stay true to themselves in a relationship. I found new strength to move through the emotional journey of ending a marriage. I garnered courage to create a new life.

A major issue in our relationship was that my ex didn't support my career ambitions and dreams. No matter which way the cards fell, he would resent things I was doing to better myself and to pursue my dreams. Plan A—the ideal plan—was for me to be at home with the kids. Plan B was for me to work 9–5 in a structured work environment. He resisted my entrepreneurial pursuits and found my schedule and ideas to be sporadic, unpredictable, and stressful. Although I recognized this early in our relationship, I was so blinded by young love that I somehow believed everything was going to work itself out. After a number of years of marriage, and having children, our differences in values and our approaches to life were also showing up as differences in our parenting. I needed to make a tough choice: either I could let my true self wither and remain true to him, or I could create a new space for the passion inside of me to drive my life and seek a complementary partner. I chose the latter. My true self wanted to be an author, coach, and trainer and to make a difference in the world.

I hold the firm belief that everything happens for a reason and that we experience challenges because of the learning and growth meant for us in this lifetime. I gave up a marriage with a wonderful man to stay true to who I am and my passion to make a difference in the world. I chose for my children to live in two homes for the rest of their lives so that they could see who I really am and learn the lessons I wanted to teach them—unaltered and unabridged. I believe that this has all happened for a reason and that it has been a gift.

Choose Today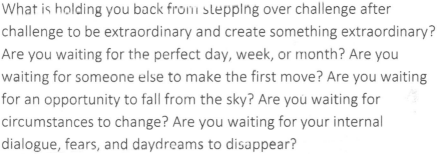

What is holding you back from stepping over challenge after challenge to be extraordinary and create something extraordinary? Are you waiting for the perfect day, week, or month? Are you waiting for someone else to make the first move? Are you waiting for an opportunity to fall from the sky? Are you waiting for circumstances to change? Are you waiting for your internal dialogue, fears, and daydreams to disappear?

It's likely that a number of limiting beliefs are inhibiting your ability to step over challenges and generate success. Everyone has these limiting beliefs because we're human. They're recorded in our minds and they play over and over. Sometimes we can hear them and sometimes we can't. Is there something that someone said to you as a child like, "You can't do that," and unknowingly you adopted this recording into your subconscious? When any obstacle comes up, whether little or big, that recording starts playing in the back of your mind: "I can't do that." Perhaps the recording is something like, "People who are successful are selfish, egotistical, and money hungry." Do you have an underlying belief that it isn't moral to be successful? Maybe you have a recording that says, "I'm not special," or "I'm not worthy," or "I'm not smart enough."

What are some of the recordings that are holding you back?

_____

_____

_____

_____

_____

_____

_____

_____

_____

Whatever's holding you back, it's time to get up, put your big girl/boy panties on, and step up. When you let your insecurities, laziness, fear, or whatever it is get in the way of you looking after yourself and contributing to others, you're playing small and selling out on the difference you could be making. Get over yourself. Look after yourself by putting the oxygen mask on first. Then get out there and make a difference. Every moment and every day that you play small is another day that passes where you're living in your own little bubble.

The funny and ironic thing is people often think that people who are playing big games and doing extraordinary things are self-absorbed and selfish. Often, the opposite is true. In her book *Think*, Lisa Bloom talks about how people focus on the gossip and drama published about Angelina Jolie rather than her extraordinary philanthropic commitment and accomplishments. People with big names are often people who have chosen the hard work and done the hard work to step over challenges. They're people playing big games to make a big difference. These are people who have the courage to step up, take action, stick out, risk public criticism, and stand for something.

If you're watching the world turn 'round, acting like an extra in the movie or an observer in the stands, and complaining about how other people should be making better decisions or making more of a difference, then you're the one who's being self-absorbed and selfish. It's high time that we all popped the bubble that surrounds us and take a good look at the real challenges that are in our communities and in the world. Rather than complaining about the small challenges in our lives and complaining about other people, we need to start taking action to contribute anything and everything that we possibly can to the real world around us. Guaranteed, our own challenges will disappear as we get connected to the true happiness and love that emerges from contributing.

More than ever, we're at a crisis in this world with people (children and adults) glued to screens and unable to effectively communicate and socialize, people suffering from cancer because of dangerous shifts in culture and lifestyle, people killing each other in underdeveloped and developed countries, and more. We need leaders, coaches, and mentors of all kinds in all areas. We need extraordinary managers in workplaces, extraordinary health professionals, extraordinary owners and directors in business. We need extraordinary people in all areas who operate in a generous, diligent, ethical, and socially responsible manner. Our world needs more people to step over the challenges of life in order to get things done and create extraordinary results.

Get 'Er Done

"If you spend too much time thinking about a thing, you'll never get it done."

BRUCE LEE

We all have things on our to-do list that just don't get done. Let's face it: the items can be little or big. Sometimes they're on our mental to-do list, and other times they make it to our physical to-do list. Sometimes the little things are actually big, and sometimes the big things are actually little. Here's the good news: it's a mental game and you can come out the winner.

Getting things done creates momentum. Who do you know that seems to have trouble following through, or forgets to complete tasks, or gets distracted, or makes goals that fall by the wayside? Let's be honest, are you that person?

You've probably noticed many things where you've spent way more time and energy thinking about getting something done than it took to actually get it done. Yes, "get 'er done" isn't a new concept. You know this. I know you know it. So what's getting in the way?

Be Chill

This is an eye opener because the paradox in this whole deal is that you'll actually chill by getting things done. Do you know how wound up you get because of the things you aren't getting done? We waste an incredible amount of emotional and physical energy feeling guilty, depressed, frustrated, and even angry about the things we don't get done. And we often don't even realize it's happening. People who get the important things done in life are often calmer, more confident, and more generous. They feel productive and accomplished at home, with family and friends, in their work, health-wise, etc. If you also get the things done you need and want to, you can actually enjoy your free time. When you take time to relax and chill, you will really feel chill.

There's a big world out there. When you take on the little things in life, it creates momentum to take on bigger and bigger and bigger things in the community and in the world. When we pretend like we're small and don't matter, there's no opportunity to make a difference. When we start living up to our potential, we can even impress ourselves with what we're capable of.

In the neighborhood where the kids' dad lives—my former home and crescent—a number of different neighbors had commented over the years and at different times to me, in completely different conversations, that they wanted to create a block party. One neighbor decided to just do it. He spoke with a few other neighbors and asked if they would be up for helping him to organize the event—and, of course, they were. They had a block party with the streets blocked off, BBQs cooking, and kids playing in the crescent. The neighbors were chatting and the party continued after the official end time. Now neighbor kids walk in and out of each other's homes, which didn't happen before. And a map was created and distributed with the names and contact information of all the families in the area. It can be difficult to put your finger on the full value and impact of this event. How do you identify how this shifted the sense of community and cooperation? The old saying, "It takes a village to raise a child," is so true.

Start Now!

Go donate blood—save a life! Register your child in piano—unleash her/his creative mind! Organize a block party—create community and prevent the neighbor kid from ending up on the streets! Install a low-flush toilet in your home—reduce your squandering of one of our planet's most critical resources! Volunteer as a Big Brother or Big Sister—give the precious gift of your time and love! Organize your closet—create some free mind space so that you can get something else done!

During a conversation with my dad about writing this book, I admitted, "I think I've been waiting for the perfect time to write. I've been waiting for a beautiful, peaceful day when I have a chunk of time—like eight hours—to just sit back and write. The reality is it's going to have to be a night from 9 to 11 p.m. with dishes sitting in the sink and laundry piled in a heap across the hallway."

There's no perfect time to start a project or keep on keeping on a project. I started writing this book by capturing notes of my thoughts in my phone and in small notebooks. Over the months as I continued to write, there were times when I was sitting on the sidelines at the playground with my laptop writing, squinting to find the cursor on the screen and defy the glare of the shadows. There were times when I was sitting in the middle of the public library while the kids picked out books, editing a chapter that I had printed.

Building on momentum is wonderful—and there will be times when some or all momentum has been lost and will need to be found again. There were times when I avoided writing for weeks or even months at a time. Even though I had started the project, I needed to get myself going again.

Sometimes what's required is putting what needs to be done right in front of you—literally. When I had boxes sitting in the basement to sort through, it was really easy to leave them in the basement. Out of sight, out of mind, right? One day, I hauled all of the boxes upstairs and stacked them in my office, which is the first room you see when you enter my home. In fact, I did that a few days before I was expecting colleagues over to the house for a meeting. Despite the fact that I didn't want to deal with the boxes, and there were lots of other things to do, the boxes sitting in my office right in front of my face meant that they became front and center.

What have you been holding off on doing because you're waiting for the perfect time? How are you going to build momentum?

In the first column below, make a list of 10 things you've been avoiding. Leave the second column blank.

1. _____   _____

2. _____   _____

3. _____   _____

4. _____   _____

5. _____   _____

6. _____   _____

7. _____   _____

8. _____   _____

9. _____   _____

10. _____   _____

Stop Ducking Out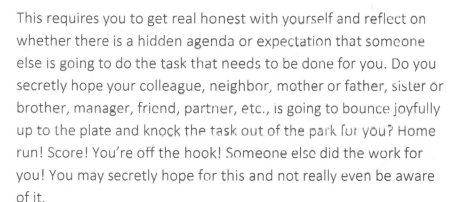

This requires you to get real honest with yourself and reflect on whether there is a hidden agenda or expectation that someone else is going to do the task that needs to be done for you. Do you secretly hope your colleague, neighbor, mother or father, sister or brother, manager, friend, partner, etc., is going to bounce joyfully up to the plate and knock the task out of the park for you? Home run! Score! You're off the hook! Someone else did the work for you! You may secretly hope for this and not really even be aware of it.

This is not to say that you need to take care of everything. It would be a big mistake to believe this is necessary or desirable. There are many things that we think we need to take care of that we could actually allow others to assist us with and give them the opportunity and gift of contributing to us. However, if you're secretly hoping to weasel out of something that you need to get done, you may as well just get it done rather than keep crossing your fingers and hoping.

Acknowledge the Impact

I met with my book coach, Dr. Denis Cauvier, months ago, and he asked me why I thought it was so important to write this book. Would it really matter if it didn't get done? I told him that I talk with people all the time who express how unhappy or unfulfilled they are. They're caught in the rat race. They're tired and/or unhealthy. They wish they were in a fulfilling partnership with their spouse. They want to get more done in life and contribute to a bigger cause. Dr. Cauvier asked me if I actually believed that my message would create a shift for people. With tears in my eyes, I said, "Yes." He then gave me some pretty direct coaching. He said, "Stop being selfish, Kara. By keeping your message inside of you, you're being selfish." I responded by saying, "That's right. I just need to get it done. My dad would say, 'Shit or get off the pot.'"

Make a powerful choice to get something done. Many of us tell ourselves and others each day that we're going to do things. Often, we have no intention of actually doing these things. Sometimes we think we might do it, and we say we will do something—and not act on what we said because that's okay in society. Everyone says they're going to do things and don't.

What goes hand in hand with making this powerful choice to get something done is getting real and acknowledging the impact of not getting it done. Look at the consequences of not getting done what you need or want to. They may be tangible consequences. They may be emotional consequences. They may have an impact on others. In Canada, if you haven't raked your leaves before it snows, either you end up raking heavy, wet leaves after the first light snowfall (if you get the chance) or you end up trying to scrape the mushy, matted leaves off the ground before they kill your grass in the spring after the snow has melted.

Sometimes you need to dig deep to see the consequences. And sometimes you need to be honest with yourself in a way that you haven't been. If you don't exercise, the impacts may include not having enough energy to play with your kids, your clothes not fitting, feeling grumpy and down and tired, being unfocused in your work, and spending more money on fast food, ultimately leading to health issues.

If you really want to look at the impact of not getting something done, ask someone who's directly impacted by your inaction. Listen openly, with deep curiosity, and without an ounce of defensiveness. We're often so caught up in our own world that we forget about how we impact those around us. We fail to recognize how far-reaching the effect of our inaction is.

Manufacture a Deadline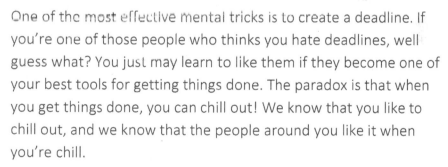

One of the most effective mental tricks is to create a deadline. If you're one of those people who thinks you hate deadlines, well guess what? You just may learn to like them if they become one of your best tools for getting things done. The paradox is that when you get things done, you can chill out! We know that you like to chill out, and we know that the people around you like it when you're chill.

In chatting with Dr. Cauvier about the progress of this book, he gently suggested that picking a date for a completed manuscript would be a good idea. Dr. Cauvier is an international author, speaker, and consultant, so it's fair to say that he knows a thing or two about getting things done. Dr. Cauvier knows that when you set a deadline, especially when you say it to someone else, you instantly become more committed and accountable.

The deadline needs to be a balance of what's realistic and what's out of your comfort zone. Set a deadline that puts you into action and pushes you out of your comfort zone. Make sure you're internally committed to the deadline rather than just throwing out a deadline for the sake of it. Give some thought to the steps you need to take in order to meet the deadline. (See the next section "Tackle the Mini Tasks" in this chapter.)

If you're embarrassed to have friends or family over to your home because of the disorganization, invite them for the next special occasion to push yourself to get done what you've been avoiding. If you've been meaning to return something to someone or do a favor that you promised, text, call, or email that person and say when you're going to do it by to make the commitment tangible. If you've been meaning to mail something, contact that person to get their address—s/he will wonder why you asked for the address if you don't send anything!

Even if you're not sure how or when you're going to get the thing accomplished, create a deadline or commitment anyway. Too often we overanalyze how we're going to get something done—the steps we need to take, the challenges we think we'll face, the resources we don't have. When you decide to bring a pet or a baby or a new car or first home into your life (yes, I realize that these are not entirely similar examples, but roll with me here), you certainly don't have all of the information as to what it is going to take to care for this new acquisition. But you decide to do it, and you figure it out one step at a time.

In the list you created in the "Start NOW!" section, using the second column, write a deadline for each of the tasks that you've been avoiding.

Tackle the Mini Tasks

There are many to-do tasks that involve mini tasks in order to fully complete them. Subconsciously, we can get overwhelmed with tasks because we haven't broken the task into mini tasks. If you need to get a process started, like hiring someone for a household or business task, take the first step of reviewing some classified ads and sending some emails. If you need to get a stain out of something, you may need to soak it first. If you want to register your child in an activity, maybe the first step is to speak to other parents to get ideas and recommendations or submit an online registration form.

We can become consumed with analyzing which mini task to begin with. Just take a first action. There are lots of times when it doesn't even matter which first mini task to tackle. We just need to take a first step. If you're cleaning your basement, it may be a matter of contacting a family member to request that s/he remove their items from the space. Or it may be a matter of borrowing a shop vac from someone. If we get going on one mini task, there's less thinking to be done. It's more a matter of one foot in front of the other.

What mini tasks are you committed to getting done tomorrow?

_____

_____

_____

_____

_____

In the case of a large project, the same mini task may simply need to be repeated and repeated in a diligent way. I told my dad that I had decided of my own volition to send my coach two to three pages of the book at a time. He could decide whether to read it or not, but at least I would be getting a chunk of writing done and submitted—and feel accountable to someone. My dad said, "That makes sense to me. Like they say, Dolly, the best way to eat an elephant is one bite at a time."

At one point, I decided to scrub about 800 square feet of the grout on my tile flooring with a toothbrush to get it clean and back to its original color. In my house, I wanted to tear up all of the tiles and replace them with hardwood flooring. My partner couldn't understand why I would want to tear up perfectly good tile that's a neutral color. He asked some curious questions (and yes, he was genuinely curious and not judgmental) about why I wanted to proceed in doing this. Finally we discovered through the conversation that the thing I disliked about the tile was that it didn't feel clean. The previous owners had a number of pets. When I moved into the house, I had the carpets cleaned by one of the best carpet cleaning companies in the city. I scrubbed the grout in the bathroom floor. But the tile on the main floor was not something I had cleaned yet. So, lo and behold, one section at a time, I began to clean the 800-square-foot section of grout with a toothbrush—10–15 minutes at a time every few days.

The challenge with waiting for a dedicated chunk of time to get 'er done all at once is that we end up forfeiting small amounts of time that could have been used to make progress on a mini task. The classic complaint of "I don't have enough time" often emerges when we have an idea or expectation of the amount of time and circumstances we think we need in order to take on the full task.

Shout It Out

Make a public declaration of what you're committed to getting done. This creates an extra level of accountability. We're human beings with fragile egos. For some odd reason, we can tolerate disappointing ourselves on a regular basis, but heaven forbid, we do not want to look bad in front of other people. We're more likely to push ourselves to get something done if we think we're going to look bad in front of someone else for not keeping our word.

In working on this book, I had to force myself to start telling people that I was writing a book. When they asked me, "What do you do for work?" I was focusing on the other professional endeavors I'm involved in. I wouldn't mention that I was writing a book. As soon as my partner started telling his family that I was writing a book, it became real. Who wants to be known as the girl who said she was writing a book and then fell off the tracks? A fear of losing face can certainly be used to your own advantage.

Another element of public declaration is using powerful language for your commitments. Cut out words like "try" and "might" and "maybe" and "kind of." Talk about what you're getting done in a way that shows your commitment. Don't say, "if"; say "when." For example, rather than saying, "If I lose 20 pounds this year..." Say, "When I lose 20 pounds this year..." Many of us talk about things we're trying to get done. If we're really committed to getting 'er done, we'll take an action. The action will either be effective or ineffective and take us closer to our desired outcome or not. In other words, there is no "trying." There's either action or inaction—and an action is either effective or ineffective.

Take the Time

Take the necessary time to get 'er done. Notice that I didn't say "make" the time because we can't make time. Time is finite. We can't expand it. The time we have is the time we have. For some reason, many of us think that time is going to one day magically expand or open up to accommodate for the things we need to get done. This doesn't happen. In each block of one minute or five minutes or 10 minutes or one hour, we have a choice in how we spend time. It's our choice how those minutes are spent, so start taking the time for your priorities and to-do list.

Time is our most precious resource. If you take the time, you're telling yourself and the world that this thing you're committed to getting done is going to get done. You may be temporarily sacrificing time with friends, time to exercise, time to play with kids, etc., to get this thing done that you've decided is important. You may block off time, or you may actually need to squeeze time in one small block of time when you can spare it. Regardless, don't even think that there's going to be a perfect time to get something done. Yes, sometimes consideration needs to be given to timing, but more often than not, the time to accomplish a task or get the ball rolling is here and now. Take the time.

Don't Feel, Just Do It

Stop expecting that things are going to be easy and that you're going to feel like doing them. Get over the fact that you "feel like" doing particular tasks. Just because you don't feel like it or because it's not easy doesn't mean that now is not the time to tackle the task. Successful people do things because the tasks need to be done, not because they feel like it. I don't feel like wiping my child's bum most days, but I do it anyway. "I don't feel like it" is just a feeling. Whether you "feel" like something or not is irrelevant when it comes to whether it would be beneficial to do. Whether you "feel" motivated or "feel" lazy, it is just a feeling. I guarantee if you go for a walk and get some fresh air that you will "feel" better after you do so. But if you don't, you may continue to feel tired, lazy, or whatever else you feel.

When I was focused on cleaning the grout of my tile flooring, friends, neighbors, and family came over and commented on how hard it must be and how long it would take to scrub line by line with a toothbrush. By that time, I had accepted that this was what needed to be done. I wanted to love my floor. And the truth was, it would be a heck of a lot easier and cheaper (and easier on the environment) to clean the grout than to rip up the tile. In fact, my partner had emphasized how much easier cleaning the grout would be than (him) ripping up the tile! So with my environmentally friendly cleaning paste in one hand, and my daughter's old pink toothbrush in the other hand, I took on one patch of grout at a time. It wasn't easy and I didn't necessarily feel like it, but it was what it was.

There are many nights when I don't feel like working out. I tend to work out at night after the kids are in bed. Sometimes it's at 12:30 a.m. after I've had a full day with the kids and worked for a few hours after they're in bed. I have a few basic pieces of equipment, and I have a few exercise routine options that vary in length from 20 minutes to an hour. This is what I have set up so that exercise is always easy and accessible. It's what works for me. There are certainly nights when I would much rather fall into bed, or have a glass of wine, or have a bubble bath. However, I stop myself from even thinking about the things I would rather do because it's not important. I have committed that my health is a priority, so the thing to do is exercise regularly. That's it. That's all. I head downstairs and begin my workout even though I don't feel like it.

What makes things hard is all the energy we put into telling ourselves and others how hard it is and how much we don't want to do something. If you saved a dog from a burning building, I don't think the person interviewing you for your heroism would focus on how hard you thought it was going to be before you ran into the burning building, or whether you felt like doing it or not. There are some things in life that we just do. And the more that we take on in life without indulging in our feelings, the drama, and our resistance, the more things get done because they're what need to get done.

Identify Distractions

We tend to think of distractions and being distracted as negative and get down on ourselves for letting them overcome us. Sometimes it's a passive annoyance with ourselves that sounds like, "Ugh. I just can't seem to get that done. There's too much going on." Sometimes it's a more fervent anger with ourselves that sounds like, "It's my own fault. I keep doing other things even though I know I shouldn't." We may even go so far as to subconsciously or consciously call ourselves weak, or a flavor of weak, because we allow ourselves to get distracted.

The key is to be straight with yourself about distractions. The more you resist being distracted, the more you'll be distracted. And when you pretend that you're not letting yourself be distracted, then it's a step backward in coming to grips with the reality of the situation in order to make a different choice. When you acknowledge your tendency to be distracted and be clear about what you're allowing yourself to be distracted by, the closer you are to the real truth.

Accept the existence of distractions. There will be distractions that come up and there will be distractions that you create, whether you create them consciously or subconsciously. We all do it because we're all human. The good news is that you know best what your distractions are, and like other people in this world who get things done, you can learn to accept and conquer distractions.

We need to distinguish a true distraction from something that needs to get done. Eating chocolate and watching television are distractions. Cooking and working out and doing chores are just things that need to get done. They're productive. When we choose to work out, it's a necessity to keep our bodies healthy and balanced. But excessive workouts can be a distraction. Grocery shopping is something that needs to get done. But excessive grocery shopping, or shopping in general, can be a distraction.

When I have a few days to focus on writing, there are also other things I need to be getting done—other work, housework, fitness, social time with friends, etc. It's all important and it all needs to get done. When I choose to go for a walk with a girlfriend (multitasking), I don't get down on myself for getting distracted because, in this case, it's not a true distraction. I acknowledge that there was another priority that I needed to take care of. By acknowledging that going for a walk isn't a true distraction, there's no need for me to waste energy on getting mad at myself for being distracted. I would be wasting energy that I could be using to write. In fact, spending time on my priority of exercising creates a need for me to be more efficient in getting my writing done.

Don't Make Yourself Wrong

This point would be worthy of a chapter on its own, but let's see what we can do here in a nutshell. When we fail to meet our own benchmarks, standards, and expectations, we're usually the first to put ourselves down. We're our own worst critics. We chastise ourselves and then get into a funk because we make out like we're stupid, lazy, worthless, etc. What stops us in moving forward in completing tasks is that we get down on ourselves for having failed at a portion of the task—an interim deadline, unsatisfactory work on a portion of the project, inability to locate needed materials, negative feedback, etc. The key to moving forward after not producing a result is to set another benchmark and to look at what it would take to meet it.

If I don't finish writing a chapter one day because I chose to go for a walk with a girlfriend, go grocery shopping, and visit a family member in the hospital, then I simply acknowledge that I didn't finish the chapter. Provided that exercising, grocery shopping, and visiting were legitimate priorities, then the situation is what it is. I focus on the facts of the situation, rather than making myself wrong. What I will look at doing is making time in my schedule the next day for writing. For example, I may reschedule an appointment that I had booked for the next day, and that is not a priority, so that I can complete the chapter.

Stop beating yourself up. If athletes made themselves out to be failures every time they made a mistake or fell short of a goal, they would never make the Olympics. We beat ourselves down so often to the point that we cannot peel ourselves off the ground to keep plugging away. We lose excitement and steam and decide things are too hard, or that we are not cut out for it, or it's not the right time. Rather than beating yourself up, simply look at whether you got something done or not. Make a new deadline with a stronger commitment and better plan to achieve it if you didn't.

My coach Dr. Cauvier also knows about failure to perform. When he asked me about the deadline I was setting for my completed manuscript, he didn't bring attention to the fact that I hadn't even come close to meeting the first manuscript deadline that I'd set with him. It had come and passed. He likely knew that I was fully aware of having completely failed at meeting the deadline. He only asked me for a new deadline.

Embrace Imperfection

There's freedom in letting go of the notion that a task or project needs to be perfect. In making hamburgers one day, my son asked me if he was getting it perfect as he scooped the raw beef mixture onto the pan and shaped it into a patty. This was not a coincidence, as his teacher had just reported to me the previous day with a smile that everything at school was going "really well" — except that he seemed to want to get things perfect and that he would get frustrated when he didn't. While we were making hamburgers, my son and I talked about how some things do need to be perfect. Other things just need to get done. And he needs to learn which is which. Performing heart surgery needs to be perfect. Making hamburger patties just needs to get done.

It wasn't a coincidence that, as I was writing this chapter, my partner was working on completing a renovation project in the basement of his home in another city. His lack of availability and freedom (time, financial, and emotional) to fully move in with me (in the same city as his work) was hinging completely on finishing this project. He needed to finish the renovations to free up his weekends, which he had been spending on the project for over a year. He needed to rent out the space to generate cash flow in order to contribute to the home that we would be living in together. He needed to let go of his home emotionally in order to be present and to focus on creating our new family together.

One Saturday night, as he was in one city and I was in another, we were talking on the phone about the progress he had made on the renovations that day and the progress I had made on writing this book. I shared this piece with him about getting things perfect. He asked for an example of something that needs to be perfect. I said that it's important for people to decide for themselves how perfect something needs to be before they can let go of it. I then asked him if his plumbing and electrical was in the place where he could pursue booking an inspection in order to get his permits that coming week. He reflected and stated that there were a few oddball tasks that he needed to take care of himself and then he could hire a plumber to come in and hook up the water lines. He had unconsciously been thinking that only he could perfect the plumbing and electrical. He recognized that he could let go of part of the task.

Is there something you're holding onto because you are attached to an idea of what perfect is? We waste time and energy thinking about what would make something perfect and working to make sure it's perfect. We continue to add extra steps to extend a task or project unnecessarily. We're often hesitant to allow people to help or to delegate the task. In the end, we take more time and energy to get 'er done or we don't get 'er done at all. There's an impact on us, and there's often a direct or indirect impact on those around us. Whether it's putting together photo albums or updating a resume or tending to the backyard or putting together a fun weekend, sometimes we just need to get something done. It will be perfect the way it is, and perfect the way it isn't. Our fantasy of perfect only exists in our own mind.

Chill 214

Get Going

When we're inactive, we're not contributing. We get bogged down by our own thoughts, drama, and small details. Take action—get 'er done. One action leads to another action. Little things lead to big things. Imagine what this world would be if we were all in action and living to our full potential. Wow! Can you even imagine?

Consider what you haven't been getting done. Don't get consumed by justifying why you haven't been getting 'er done. Review the sections in this chapter and write down what you're now committed to getting done and how you're going to get 'er done.

1. Be Chill

_____

_____

_____

_____

2. Start NOW!

_____

_____

_____

_____

3. Stop Ducking Out

_____

_____

_____

_____

4. Acknowledge the Impact

_____

_____

_____

_____

5. Manufacture a Deadline

_____

_____

_____

_____

6. Tackle the Mini Tasks

_____

_____

_____

_____

7. Shout It Out

_____

_____

_____

_____

8. Take the Time

_____

_____

_____

_____

9. Don't Feel, Just Do It

_____

_____

_____

_____

10. Identify Distractions

_____

_____

_____

_____

11. Don't Make Yourself Wrong

_____

_____

_____

_____

12. Embrace the Imperfection

_____

_____

_____

_____

Wonderful Women's Stories

"What we women need to do, instead of worrying about what we don't have, is just love what we do have."

CAMERON DIAZ

It is an honor and a privilege to share the following stories of wonderful women with you. Julie, Kate, Alice, and Laurie have been generous in sharing the challenges they've faced. Their accomplishments and wisdom are extraordinary. What these women have moved through and achieved throughout their lives thus far is incredible. I chose to interview these women for four reasons: they've all made courageous choices; they're a stand for creating happiness and love in their lives; they give and give and give; and they're consistently smiling and being positive.

Julie's Story

Julie was a driven, Type A personality, and a people pleaser growing up. She always tried to please her dad. In university, she studied science and microbiology. Julie then took an internship in Washington, DC, in a lab, which she thought would please her dad.

As Julie was working in the lab in DC, she felt herself becoming very unhappy. She didn't like working in the lab, but she was doing it anyway. The 9/11 attacks had happened only months prior, and there was a heavy fog of stress all around the lab and the city. She remembers washing her face one day and looking in the mirror. She saw the sad face of a woman who she didn't recognize in the mirror looking back at her. Julie thought to herself, "If I die tomorrow, I'm going to die unhappy. And I will not have made a difference." She recognized that she couldn't keep up trying to please her dad. Things needed to change. She could see that she needed to start looking at what she wanted to do for herself. Even if she couldn't picture the whole staircase of where she was going in life and what her purpose was, she needed to start taking the first steps.

Julie knew that she loved communication, skin, science, and teaching. She found a job working with L'Oréal, educating employees in the company and bringing a scientific flare to the L'Oréal brand, which allowed her to tap into all of these interests. While working with L'Oréal, she fell in love with a handsome man, a physician 22 years her elder, and he asked her to marry him. She moved across the country to be with him, but she found it difficult to find a new job that was as interesting and fulfilling as the one with L'Oréal.

Contemplating how to further her career in the new city, Julie began to recognize that there was a niche in the skin care industry. She noticed that dermatologists know about skin health but are so busy seeing patients that they don't have time to educate people. Estheticians have a love for skin and have time to spend with people, but they don't have a deep educational background. She decided to create a business around the science of skin. She believed at that time that her purpose was to help people with their skin.

Julie's business thrived, but her relationship with her husband began to fall apart. Julie believes that there's always a tipping point before a relationship falls apart, and she remembers exactly when that was for her. One day, she called her husband and said, "I don't know what to do anymore. I don't know how to take our relationship further. Things aren't working. We need help. We have a problem. Would you come to counselling with me?" He responded, "I don't have a problem. You have a problem. Go get fixed." She saw clearly that she had done everything she could. A relationship is a two-way street, and she saw that if one way was closed, she needed to move on.

Julie began to recognize that her husband had come into her life for a "season and a reason." He had helped her lay the foundations for her business. He was also helping her to recognize that money doesn't buy happiness. She lived in a castle and could do and buy anything she wanted, but she was miserable. When she shared with her husband that she wanted to end the relationship, he said, "You'll never be able to afford a life like the one I offer you." She agreed and told him that she would rather be happy.

It was a journey of strength and support building for Julie to get ready to end the marriage and move on. Julie knew she needed to be patient with becoming ready to move forward, and she knew she was going to need the strength of a community around her. She leaned on new and old friends to support her. She continued to live in the home with her husband. Julie did training through Landmark Worldwide and spent significant time exploring her spirituality. She was committed to growing herself. Given her Type A personality, she wanted a quick fix, but she held herself back. She admits, "I can see now that this was a good approach. Had I left him the day he said, 'I don't have a problem,' the process of leaving the marriage and rebuilding my life would not have gone nearly as well as it did." Julie truly experienced the power of taking one step at a time and stepping into the unknown to recreate her life.

As she continued building her business, Julie began to see that her business was not just about making money but about making a difference. Julie was experiencing the joy and fascination of truly connecting with people and of building relationships to support them. She found that her conversations with clients would move from skin to what they were dealing with in their lives. Her clients would return to let her know that they appreciated and took seriously the ideas and coaching she had given them. Her clients began sharing more deeply with her about the challenges they were facing. She could feel the difference she was making in empowering people, and she felt empowered to be doing it. She had found her purpose. Through helping people with their skin, she could come into their lives and make a difference.

Julie found that her confidence and success were growing every day. As Julie took personal and professional development courses, she repaired her relationship with her dad. This gave her the internal freedom to continue growing her business in accordance with her own direction and passion, rather than worrying about her dad's wishes. As challenges came up in her life, she found that she was able to deal with them quickly and vigorously. She would face a problem and find a solution, and/or let go of the problem. Instead of dwelling on or being stopped by problems for months or years, they became mere hiccups in her life.

In April of 2014, Julie stepped on stage to speak to an audience of 14,000 people, and in a single moment, everything that had occurred up to this point in her life made sense to her. Her studies in biology, her work in the lab, her marriage, her business, her learning with Landmark Worldwide, and her growth in spirituality had all brought her to this point. The hard work she had put in, the challenges she had faced, and the pain she had felt was all a blessing. And she was at a point where she could now make a difference in thousands of people's lives. No longer was she working one on one. There were 14,000 people sitting in front of her eager to hear what she had to say.

Julie is now connected to her true passion, which is to inspire women and to be an agent of change. She says that life is all about the small choices that we make every day. With every choice, we need to look at whether it brings us closer to what we intend to create. We need to listen to our intuition. She says life is all about doing things for the right reasons—not to please others.

She says life needs to be about keeping things simple rather than looking good. She thinks we live in a world with a lot of greed and pride and that the focus is on accumulating material possessions. Julie explains that we can't take our possessions with us when we die. She says, "Whether you drive a Toyota or a Porsche, it's going to take you where you're going. We don't need the stuff to impress, and we don't need the stuff anyway." She believes that it is way more important to find and pursue your purpose in life and to make choices daily that take you closer to fulfilling your purpose in a simple and humble way.

Julie admits that she used to believe that who she was as a person was equal to what she owned. She professes, "I was an obnoxious bitch. I used to get a high from being rich because I felt superior to others. But it was unhealthy and stressful. It was hard to keep up." She used to think that having a successful, extraordinary life was about having a good job, having lots of money, and having people look up to her. She used to think that people would want to be friends with her because she had a lot of money.

Julie's authenticity has skyrocketed. She's not one person in one setting and another person in the next setting. She's the same person speaking on stage as she is speaking with friends. She shares about her breakthroughs and about her challenges. She owns her success, but she isn't afraid to talk about her real problems. People say that she talks and acts the same wherever she goes and that she tells it like it is.

Three months after moving out of the home she shared with her ex-husband, Julie met her soul mate. She says, "I traded a pebble for a rock. My ex thought he was my everything and the rock in my life. But he was just a pebble. Now I have a partner who is truly my rock." Julie feels that she is loved unconditionally. Julie and her partner share the same spiritual beliefs, and they both believe that you should do whatever you need to fulfill your purpose.

Simplicity is a powerful force. Julie says that she's free, at peace, and productive now. She's able to accomplish more because she doesn't worry about what others think. She's not thinking about whether she looks good or what car to buy. She says that when you stop comparing yourself to others, it streamlines your life. She lives a busier life but a simpler one. A no-frills mantra allows her to need less stuff, which gives her space and time to foster relationships and her spirituality. Julie focuses on doing the right things for the right reasons.

Julie believes that we need to trust the process of life. Past choices and experiences need to be appreciated for the learning and growth they've brought into our life. It's powerful to look at all of our experiences as a blessing and to contemplate how they've brought us to the place where we're at, which is in line with our purpose. As long as we commit to look at our experiences as falling in line with our purpose, there's no need for guilt, resentment, regret, or anger. With a clear purpose, everything in life seems to flow more fluidly and easily.

Kate's Story

Kate is committed to her family—to her marriage and to her kids. Kate says her and her husband decided when they were dating that they would never divorce. They would stick through whatever there was to stick through. Today they live on an acreage in Western Canada and are parents to five beautiful children and open to more in the future. Kate's husband is the president of a heavy equipment business, farms a section of land, and cares for their sheep, cattle, and horses at home in his spare time.

Kate began studying science in university and was admitted into veterinary medicine after two years. She says that she focused on academics in school, had a goal, and didn't "party ever, at all, in life." When she graduated as a doctor, she planned on pursuing a residency in equine medicine in the U.S.

Kate and her husband were dating at the time and decided that they needed to make a choice about their lives' direction together. He was willing to follow her south to do the residency, but they thought it made more sense to put his career first and for him to pursue the family business, given that he was likely to be the provider going forward. Kate says that she decided she could always go back to school after having kids. Kate did a residency in a nearby small town, and although it wasn't glamorous, she says that she's thankful because it was an incredible learning experience.

After working in the residency for a year, Kate became pregnant. In that year, she miscarried twice, and the order of her priorities changed. Originally she thought she would work for some time and then would have kids. She always took it for granted that she could have kids anytime, but she was seeing that there was an expiry date on her ability to have children. Yet there was no expiry date on the ability to go to school or work. It became clear to Kate that having kids was really important to her. Kate and her husband had their first child, and every two years after they've had another. They didn't have a master plan as to how many children they wanted to have—they've just taken things one step at a time, one child at a time, and have always been thankful for the gift of giving life to another child.

Kate admits straight up that marriage isn't easy and that being a mom isn't easy. However, she emphasizes how grateful she is that her husband has taken on being the provider for the family with true dedication. He works long hours and is rarely home for supper. He travels for work approximately six or seven overnights per month. She says gratefully and empathetically, "Even when he's tired from work, he comes home and does an amazing job of making it a priority to be with the family. He'll suggest we take the kids swimming even when I know that he's exhausted."

Kate's husband has a Grade 10 education, works with his hands, and is a welder. Kate laughs sheepishly and says that when she was dating her husband, she broke up with him and told him that if she was to consider marrying him he needed to go to school, get more exercise, and be more fun. She says that on top of working 14-hour days, he began swimming in the morning and taking night classes to complete a high school science course.

After a few weeks of him trying to win her back, Kate came to her senses and saw again how incredible her husband is. Now he works in an office all day, running businesses and working with numbers. Kate humbly admits that she used to think that someone would only be a welder if there was nothing else they could do. She now sees how practical, intelligent, and dedicated her husband is. She says she's grateful for how differently they think and says that they make a great team. She also says that she now appreciates his quiet personality, and she enjoys that he has no need to be the center of attention.

When asked how she gets through the day, Kate laughs and says that quiet time is the secret to happiness. She says that everyone needs a nap or at least quiet time. She says they focus on having a routine as a family. She says they also limit screen time (television, movies, computer, tablets, phone, etc.) for the kids. They don't have cable television. They do have some videos, which enables her and her husband to know what the kids are watching. The kids don't have their own Internet access; they can use her laptop in the kitchen so that she knows what they're viewing. Kate says that she notices that screen time changes the kids' personality and that once they get going on screen time, it's hard to stop them. Their daily routine is filled with play with each other and with the animals outside. Quiet time either involves napping or reading books.

Another decision Kate and her husband made when they were dating was not to put their kids in hockey. She says that it sounds funny, but basically it means that they were very clear that their life wasn't going to revolve around their kids' activity schedules and that they weren't going to run around like crazy. She says they keep activities simple. Their kids participate in the same activities at the same times. For instance, two of the children have piano at the same time and at the same place during the week. Kate and her husband are looking at introducing one more activity but in the same way: same activity, same time, and same place.

When asked how she stays positive, Kate shares that her kids are so thankful, happy, and fun. She says that their family focuses on keeping things simple so that life stays light. For instance, they don't host birthday parties where 10 children and a princess come to tear around the house. She says they invite a family over to celebrate. The children play, and the adults visit. The birthday child receives one gift from the visiting family and one gift from their family. This teaches the kids that relationships are more important than the frills and material things.

Kate emphasizes that they don't focus on material wealth or having the latest and greatest things. She says her and her husband don't want to spoil the kids, and don't want the kids to be snobby. "We don't worry about having the newest vehicle. We just drive something that's practical and that works," she says. Their credit cards are locked in the barn with their guns. They have a budget and an allotted amount of cash set aside for every two-week period. Kate says that they don't do a lot of extravagant things. For vacation, they'll drive to the neighboring province to stay with her parents at their vacation home there. She says she likes to drink her coffee and chat with her husband as he drives while the kids read their books and sleep in the back. They don't go to Hawaii or Disney. She says she can only imagine flying with kids would be stressful.

Key values for Kate and her husband are acceptance of all people and appreciation of community. Kate's younger brother has Down syndrome, so as she was growing up, she learned the importance of acknowledging and honoring the value everyone brings to the community. As her brother grew up, her parents pushed hard for him to be included. He attended mainstream school, attended university, and lived in the dorms. Kate likes to shop at the Salvation Army. She explains to the kids that the Salvation Army employs people with disabilities and encourages people to reuse items. Kate's family attends community family dances where the kids experience the joy of all kinds of people—

including people with disabilities and in wheelchairs—having fun, and connecting.

When asked how she looks after herself, Kate responds by saying that she's thankful for the family support they have. Although her mom still works full-time at the university, her mother-in-law has been generous over the years and takes the children on Fridays. That works for both Grandma and Kate. Since some of the children are in school, it's only been two or three kids at a time for Grandma, so Kate would spend Fridays doing things that make her happy like going to the spa or shopping for clothes for herself. Sometimes she goes grocery shopping on Fridays. Prior to her father-in-law falling ill, Grandma and Grandpa would have the kids sleep over three Fridays per month, and Kate and her husband would have a date night.

Kate admits that there are moments when she wishes she had more time for herself, but she quickly reminds herself that she'll have lots of time to herself when her kids are older. She is incredibly grateful for this time with her kids. She says you can't have kids when you're 50, but you can go back to work when you're 50. She says that her competitiveness has her always looking for a challenge. She learned and grew from the challenge of her studies, but she says she's now shifted her focus to learning and growing from the challenge of caring for her family. Kate looks at being a mom as the ultimate challenge. "It's not about me," she emphasizes. She says that by nature she is not an organized person, but being a mom of five pushes her to be organized. She's thankful for her husband fully taking on the role of provider so that she can fully take on the role of being a mom. And she is thankful for their cleaner, who now comes for five hours on Fridays.

Kate focuses on being thankful. She says that her faith has given her stability, and the ability to be thankful for what she has— not material wealth but the things of substance. She looks around her new home with a dream kitchen, granite countertops, marble floors, crystal light fixtures, glass door knobs, new furniture, and says, "I mean, the house is beautiful. But it's really not that important to me. I actually miss living in the mobile home that we lived in while we were building this house." For Kate, her life isn't all about her. She shares passionately, "I'm always looking for how can I give? How can I serve? How can I be a blessing to someone else?"

Alice's Story

As a little girl, Alice remembers one day watching her mom standing in the grocery store and seeing her cry. She asked her mom why she was crying and her mom replied that she couldn't figure out what to buy to feed the family with the family allowance check. There had been a drought and the family had no garden and no crops. Times were tough on the farm.

Alice says that her mom gave her whole life to her husband and children. She was devoted to the family. Her mom spent her life pregnant. There were 10 living children in the family; if there was more than a year difference in age between two of the children, her mom had miscarried. Alice remembers the one thing that her mom did for herself was to wear lipstick. Her mom's friend was an Avon lady. Alice's mom would use the tiny Avon lipstick samples and wear lipstick, even out to feed the pigs and chickens. When Alice's mom was 45, she had a stroke and passed away. Everyone said when her mom died that she was always happy and always smiled.

When her mom passed away, Alice, at 15 years old in Grade 10, became a mom to five younger siblings. Alice had decided that she didn't want to be a martyr like her mom. She knew that in order for her to go to school and leave the farm, she would need to earn a scholarship; her dad wouldn't be able to afford to send her to school. So she did. She says the scholarship was like her ticket off the farm. When she left home for college, her sister was 15 and took over being the mom. Then when her third sister left home, their dad got sick and passed away. The three youngest siblings moved from the farm to be cared for by their older siblings.

In college, Alice loved studying science. She wanted to work in a hospital and wear a uniform, but she didn't want to be a nurse. She took medical laboratory science, which allowed her to study chemistry, biology, and hematology. She liked that, as a lab tech, she would interact with patients, but she wouldn't need to do the bedside care.

Alice met her husband at a college party, through her best friend in her med lab class. It was just before Christmas, a stormy, winter night in Saskatoon, and she told her friend Andrew that she wasn't coming to his party because the roads were too bad. He said, "You have to come. You're my best friend." So Alice and her roommates drove across town to the party and got stuck on his street getting there. A carload of kids had driven in from Alberta, the neighboring province. There was a guy who was also named Andrew in the group. He was fun and gregarious. Alice was shy. She remembers Andrew coming up behind her in the kitchen at the party and giving her a kiss. She found out later that he decided in that moment that he was going to marry her.

Andrew got Alice's phone number at the party, visited his parents on their farm over Christmas, and then called Alice on his way back through town after the holidays to invite her to a movie. She says, "Something deep within me must have been scared of him, even at this point. I was 21, but I took my roommate on the date with me."

The following month, Alice moved to Edmonton when her best friend was diagnosed with cancer. Andrew moved from Edmonton to Vancouver for work. He was due back to Edmonton in the spring. Andrew got Alice's new Edmonton address from their mutual friend Andrew. He wrote Alice beautiful letters in the months while he was in Vancouver. The handwriting was beautiful, and he was expressive with his thoughts. Alice and Andrew exchanged letters and then went on a date when Andrew returned to Edmonton in the spring.

Alice says that Andrew drank too much and that she was scared of him, but she loved how he taught her to have fun. They would go to parties and cabarets and have a wonderful time. Alice ended up breaking up with Andrew in August of 1974 because of his drinking. After they broke up, he drank more, and he would ride around on his motorcycle. He would be so drunk that he couldn't stop and hold the bike up at red lights, so he would keep riding around the block.

Alice thought that if she didn't take Andrew back, he was going to kill himself on the motorcycle. Alice knew that Andrew loved her. He would listen to her dreams to have a house and children, and he promised himself that they would have a house by the time they got married. They got engaged on Christmas Eve in 1974 and were married on July 31, 1976.

Andrew became violent after Alice became a mom with their first child, a daughter. "He was jealous," says Alice. Alice believes that Andrew's unresolved past exploded. As a boy growing up, Andrew had seen his dad beat his mom. When he was a toddler, he would stand in front of his mom to protect her. His dad would then beat him and say things like, "You're not even my son." Andrew had begun drinking when he was eight years old, taking alcohol at weddings or wherever he could get it. He claimed he was an alcoholic by 16. Alice admits that she thought she could save Andrew and used to think, "If I just love him enough, he will change."

Andrew and Alice were great business partners. They were running a multimillion dollar construction company together. Andrew was a dreamer and a risk-taker, and Alice would make sure that everything held together logistically and financially.

After many years of marriage and violence, Alice began seeing a counsellor. She asked her counsellor, "How do I help my kids?" He told her to grow up. He explained that her husband was most likely about four years old emotionally and that she was about six years old emotionally. Alice realized that she didn't know how to grow up. She began the journey of "Healing the Child Within," which was the program her counsellor gave her to work through. She began to get to know herself and to love herself. She learned that joy means love turned inward. She says, "When I started loving myself, I started treating myself like someone that was loveable and then modeled that for my kids."

For six years, Alice focused on keeping herself safe and the kids safe. Before bed every night, Alice would ask the question, "What is the next step?" She would wake up the next morning and the message was "Wait." She began thinking about how she could reframe this life experience that was so painful and scary into something that would make a difference for other people. One morning she woke up and asked her usual question, "What is the next step?" The message was "It's time." She told Andrew that she wanted a divorce.

Over the next few years, Alice created a new life. She watched Andrew run the business they'd built into the ground and go bankrupt. She went back to work as a lab tech, doing insurance medicals, drug testing, and other related work. The hours were flexible, which allowed her to work around the kids' schedule.

Alice chose to go back to school at age 45, to start her fourth career, which was the age at which her mom had passed away. Alice shares that this was both the most exciting and scariest time of her life. It was like starting all over again. She decided that she was going to live this half of her life for her and her mom. She began taking classes about conflict resolution and wanted to be a mediator. Her instructors told her to keep her day job and not to count on making a living as a mediator. Alice remembers thinking, "Oh, I will make it as a mediator!"

"I decided that I was going to start my own mediation practice on September 1, 1998," she says. At the end of August 1998, the medical company that she was working for sold out. Alice went home to tell her kids, and they said this was her sign to maintain her commitment to start her mediation practice the following month like she said she would. Alice says that it all happened with synchronicity. She received a small severance package from the medical company, and she was able to collect Employment Insurance, which gave her a financial cushion while she started her practice.

Alice still remembers her first paid mediation, which was for a couple that was divorcing. She billed them $150 per hour for five hours of mediation, for a total of $750. She remembers thinking that was a lot of money to charge for her services. At the same time, she had just spent $73,000 in legal fees on her own divorce. The couple was so happy with the outcome of the mediation, and only paying $750 for the divorce was a miracle. Alice admits that it took her a long time to move through her blocks around her own self-worth and to feel worthy of charging industry rates for her services.

"Now I have a very successful business and enjoy my practice more than anyone I know in the field. I choose my work and pass on any extra work to my amazing colleagues." Alice says that she loves her clients and she loves her work. She claims that she never would have found her purpose had she not been through the challenges she experienced in her marriage. She says that she needed Andrew to help her find her purpose.

Alice believes that every one of her partnership relationships has been a gift and has taught her something about human nature, the world, and herself. She says, "I have had wonderful relationships. Even the really brief ones were opportunities for learning."

Alice is grateful for her relationship with Andrew. He taught her how to have fun. She remembers riding for miles and miles and weeks and weeks on his motorcycle. In the process of their divorce, Alice found her purpose. She's also grateful for the two beautiful children they created. Alice remains close to Andrew's mom and calls her regularly. Andrew is now sober and healthy and works on road construction out of town. Alice says that Andrew has admitted that even though he has nothing in the way of finances, he's the happiest he's ever been. Alice is thankful that he's chosen to build a relationship with his grandchildren and that their children are seeing the man that Alice fell in love with.

After many years of being single, eventually Alice's kids said to her, "Mom, you should get a life." Her girlfriend had a party and said that she was going to invite a blind date for Alice. Alice was hoping it was her son's hockey coach because Alice had a real crush on him. Sure enough, it was. The two went out on a few dates afterward, but Alice says there was just no spark. "It was like kissing a brother," she says lightheartedly. Alice introduced him to her best friend.

One time Alice received a wedding invitation and decided to ask one of her male friends to go with her as her date. As he lived out of town, they'd been emailing each other regularly. Every time he would come to town, they would go out for dinner. After emailing him about the wedding invite, he phoned her back and declined the invitation. She was shattered, took it personally, and decided the friendship was over.

When she calmed herself down, Alice recognized that she needed to practice the self-reflection and communication that she teaches in her work, so she looked within herself to see what the declined invitation was really about for her. She saw that it challenged her self-worth, that if he had accepted the invitation, she would have felt worthy. She knew that no one could give her self-worth; this event was a reminder of this powerful life lesson. She was grateful for this critical reminder, so she called him back to thank him for saying no.

Alice's friend shared with her that him declining the invitation had nothing to do with her. He told her that he had taken another woman he had been dating and really cared about to a wedding. They took photos of themselves before attending the wedding, and he had planned on proposing to her, but on the way home she broke up with him. He just couldn't bring himself to go to another wedding.

Alice says this was a marked learning point where what other people say or do is rarely because of you. It's usually about something that's going on for them. Her favorite question now is "What makes you say that?" because she has learned to get curious about other people's thoughts and feelings. She says it makes you realize that people are struggling to make it through their own complex lives, and your wants and needs aren't often considered in their struggle.

Alice remembers dating one man for eight months. His daughter had the same name as Alice's daughter, and his daughter had the same birthday as Alice. But this man was very unhappy and angry with his former partner and would become irritated by small things. For example, he would complain that Alice's house was too far away. His kids were very sweet and he was a good dad, but Alice knew that the relationship wasn't for her. She continued dating him for months after she realized that this man wasn't it for her because she loved his kids. Eventually, she ended the relationship. Years later, his daughter registered in the university course that Alice teaches. Alice was reminded that it doesn't work to stay in a relationship for the wrong reasons such as loving the kids but not the parent. She says that you can maintain the relationship with a child even if a relationship doesn't last.

One partner in particular taught Alice how to let someone love her. He adored her. She says that was the gift from him. Alice learned to open her heart and let it in. When he retired, he started gambling. His friends told Alice that someone had to talk to him about the gambling and that it needed to be her. She confronted him about his choices, and he broke up with her. Alice says that another gift in this relationship was her having the courage to stand up and confront him.

Another man Alice dated was introduced to her by friends. Alice says they went out, and that on the second date, he proposed to her. He wanted to take care of her. Even though the idea was appealing, she says that he was so boring. Even though she recognized immediately that he wasn't the type of man she was looking for, she went out with him a few more times. She was worried about disappointing her friends. Alice admitted to herself that continuing to date this man was not serving herself, him, or her friends. Her sister reminded her how precious time is. Alice ended their relationship. She introduced him to her cousin and he found her cousin boring.

Alice says that her last partner showed her what it was like to be with a sober alcoholic—a dry drunk. She admits that she had always wondered what would've happened had she stayed with Andrew and had he sobered up. Her last partner shed some light on this question for her, since he was a former alcoholic. She says, "He doesn't have the joy of sobriety." Alice says that she can see the parallels between this partner and Andrew. His and Andrew's birthdays were only four days apart, and he was jealous of Alice spending time with her grandchild (as Andrew had been jealous when she was a mom).

After this partner cheated on her and they broke up, Alice said to him, "Go be happy. Have a good life." Alice worked to heal and forgive him. She says, "That was a lesson from him. When I say I've forgiven someone, I'll be tested. You have to really mean it when you wish someone well. I didn't really mean it when I said it to him." Alice saw his car parked down her street and realized that he was dating one of her neighbors. This was the test. Every time Alice saw his car down the street, she focused on forgiveness and being grateful that he was at that house and not hers. She wanted to be with someone she could trust. Discovering true forgiveness opened her heart.

Alice admits that after healing from her last relationship, she's now starting to notice attractive men her age and has become interested in dating again. She wants someone to sit with on the porch and rock in rocking chairs together. She's put two rocking chairs on her porch so that they're ready and waiting; she believes in taking action to attract what she wants in life. She wants to enjoy spending the money that she's worked so hard to earn and save. (In fact, her kids tell her to spend all of her money.) She wants more play time for her and more play time with her grandkids.

Key words of wisdom from Alice include: women need to ask lots of questions; women need to trust their instincts to judge character; and women need to write their own stories. "If you can dream it, you can achieve it. Life is all about choice," advises Alice.

Her sister said many years ago, "This isn't a rehearsal, Alice. This is your life."

Alice talks about her niece, who's dealing with making life choices. Her niece received a full university scholarship, just graduated from school, got a wonderful job, and is now traveling around the world with her work. But her niece is questioning whether she is passionate about her career. Alice plans to tell her niece, "You can have as many careers as you want. You can have anything you want." Alice believes that everything happens in perfect synchronicity. If you're paying attention, the signs are always there saying, "Look here!" You just have to look.

Laurie's Story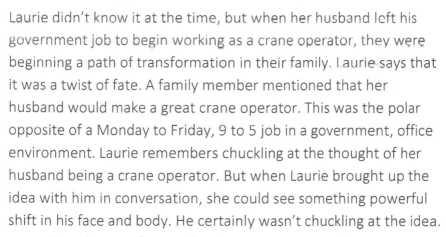

Laurie didn't know it at the time, but when her husband left his government job to begin working as a crane operator, they were beginning a path of transformation in their family. Laurie says that it was a twist of fate. A family member mentioned that her husband would make a great crane operator. This was the polar opposite of a Monday to Friday, 9 to 5 job in a government, office environment. Laurie remembers chuckling at the thought of her husband being a crane operator. But when Laurie brought up the idea with him in conversation, she could see something powerful shift in his face and body. He certainly wasn't chuckling at the idea.

Over the next few weeks, the crane operator idea came up in their conversation more and more. Finally Laurie's husband said, "Why not get more information? It doesn't hurt to ask." Off he went to inquire. He was turned down, as he had no experience in any related field. They gave him a long list of courses that he would have to complete to even be considered. He went home and registered for all of them. Laurie says that she saw a drive, desire, and excitement that she hadn't seen in her husband for over a decade, since he'd started his government position.

Laurie and her husband decided they had nothing to lose. The pay as an apprentice crane operator was about the same as he was making at the time. Her husband chose to take a year off to pursue this endeavor. When he was hired, Laurie saw a new man. He was so happy, energized, and fulfilled.

Laurie's husband began travelling as part of his work. She admits that she was in a really bad place at this time—mentally, emotionally, and physically. She sees now that she was in a hamster wheel, going through the motions day after day. Laurie thought that her life was good, that things were as good as they were going to get. When she looked around, it appeared that she had everything someone would want: the perfect marriage; perfect, healthy children; a perfect, big, and beautiful home; and a perfect, high-paying job. It didn't make sense to her that she felt so unhappy.

Laurie was both working full-time and the primary caregiver. Her husband was out of town for 10 days and then home for four days. Previously, her husband was the one who was physical and active with their two boys, who were both under six years of age at the time. He would roll around on the floor with them, play outside, get into their make-believe games, and follow whatever activity they were passionate about in the moment. While her husband traveled, Laurie was left with the boys for many days at a time on her own. She was scared for her children because she relied on her husband to be the "fun one." She didn't have it in her to do this. She was exhausted and didn't know how to be "fun." This was her awakening, and what started a transformation. It began for her children.

Laurie's life began to shift when she started doing a 25-minute workout routine in the mornings. She would get up early, go in the basement, plug in the video, and start her day in her sneakers. Laurie says, "It was hard. I'm not going to lie. I had given so much of my energy to being a mom and wife that I really felt I had nothing left to give. How was I going to add more to my life? Every morning the alarm would go off at 5:15 a.m. My world was still sleeping, and I would begrudgingly roll over and turn off the alarm. No snooze allowed. I would actually sleep in my workout clothes and put my sneakers by the bed like slippers. The night before I would set up my equipment, right down to having the workout disc in the DVD player. I also had an iPod by my bed with the song 'Stronger' by Kelly Clarkson cued up. Surrounding myself with a powerful, upbeat song made it hard to stay in that bed. Within two minutes I was up and ready to go! So much of this was the mental aspect, not the physical."

Only about one month after beginning to work out, Laurie knew that this pursuit in health and exercise was different than her other pursuits in the past. Over the previous 15 years, she had done everything to lose weight: fad diets, pills, wraps, cleanses, diet shakes filled with chemicals, starvation, and excessive exercise routines. She would count down the days until the end of the program. She would lose weight, feel terrible and exhausted, and then find the weight again. It seemed like she was always on a diet.

With this new program, Laurie was regaining vitality, and people were noticing. She was working with a coach every day online, doing a workout program that suited her and her goals, and eating real, whole foods. She realized that she hadn't actually been eating enough over the years, so she was brainwashed and depleted. Now she was eating lots of food and felt alive. People told her how great she looked.

Only two months into her journey, Laurie began to coach people in how to transform their lives by working out and eating healthier diets. Laurie was excited to help people create a spark that could become a flame. She says, "People want to be happy and healthy! Some don't know how, or some lack the motivation to do it. And that's where a coach comes in, to get you over that initial hump and keep you rolling along." Laurie was surprised to find that helping others motivated her even more. She felt even more energized and excited than when she was only working out for herself.

As Laurie reunited with her health, she began to get straight with herself about her choices at home. She did some reality checks. She began to see that there would always be dishes. There would always be dusting. There would always be floors to clean. There would always be stuff to pick up or organize. There would always be errands to run. She could do chores with her newfound energy or she could be with her kids. She says that she began to recognize that she was hiding her true sadness behind the laundry, dishes, cooking, and the million things that all moms do. The boys were growing older every day, and she wanted to truly enjoy quality time with them.

She decided to make a shift and it began with a commitment to say yes when her boys asked her to play. Previously she would have said no to them and continued doing whatever task she thought was more important at the time. She started catching herself in the middle of saying no to her boys when they asked her to play with them. She started to say yes instead—it was that simple. Laurie began to realize how many moments, days, weeks, and months she had missed enjoying these precious play times with her boys over the years. As she formed a habit of saying yes when the boys asked her to play, it became easier and easier to step away from chores and other responsibilities to be fully present and in action with her two little guys every day.

Laurie continued to see her husband happy at work, which prompted her to take a step back and look at her own career. For so many years prior, it had seemed that they were both happy with their government jobs and the security, pay, and pension that goes along with government work. But Laurie started to see more clearly, as it stared her in the face, that they'd actually been miserable, and that they'd just been going through the hamster wheel of life, doing what they thought they were supposed to do Their "good" life was about acquiring stuff, looking good, and going through the daily grind to acquire stuff and look good. She could see that they were sacrificing happiness for mediocrity.

The next transformational step was for Laurie to leave her government job. Laurie says, "At 38 years old, I thought I was crazy to think I could start over. But with the encouragement of my husband, who was also finding happiness in a new world that he was creating, I decided to take five years off to become a stay-at-home mom." Rather than driving the boys to before-school care and picking them up from after-school care, Laurie began taking them to school and picking them up from school. She says, "To be there, before and after school, for my kids—to not be frazzled trying to fit in the cooking, cleaning, grocery shopping, running from one activity to another—to be present. This was true happiness." She also had more time to pursue her new passion of coaching.

One more major shift in their lives was for Laurie and her husband to sell their 3,000-square-foot dream home—or what they thought was their dream home. They saw how much time they were spending driving to their home in the suburbs, cleaning their home, paying to heat their home, etc. Laurie admits they didn't even use all the rooms in the house. She says, "I spent weeks shopping for light fixtures for that house. I looked at light after light after light. And I ordered the lights in from New York. For some odd reason, this seemed like the most important thing in the world at the time. I was in a fog."

When Laurie got really honest with herself, she realized that she had been so unhappy in her life over the previous 10-plus years that she had continually been looking to buy and decorate a bigger home to try and fill that void. She kept thinking a new, bigger, and better home would make her happy. "Nobody wants to admit that they're actually unhappy, chasing their tail, and trying to fill a void," she says. Over the years, Laurie and her husband would buy a home, fix it up, decorate it, and sell it furnished. They became so good at this that they bought and sold home after home. Because they sold the homes furnished, they would completely start over again and again and again. Each time they bought a new house, it was bigger, and Laurie could immerse herself in fixing it up and decorating it, instead of dealing with the unhappiness in her life.

Laurie realized that she'd been hiding in this pattern for years and chose to be truly tenacious, to take the reins, and to create real happiness in life. It took deep courage for her to look at what was happening and to take personal responsibility for the pattern and her unhappiness. She recognized that this last home they had created was just not it—it wasn't saving the day. Although it looked like they had it "made in the shade" on the outside, there was still an empty void within her. In fact, Laurie shares that she didn't even want to hang pictures in the 3,000-square-foot home because something about the whole thing just didn't seem right.

"I had spent two years designing and building my dream home. Every single aspect of it. There were changes—a lot of changes. I had to get it right. This was my last shot, as we truly felt this was our forever home. The home we were going to raise our children in and be the last step to retirement. I put my heart and soul into it. It consumed me. I remember so vividly moving in and not feeling anything. Not feeling what I had hoped for. I kept waiting for the day I would be so happy in that home. It never came. Once I began to start loving me, all of me, who I was and what I was capable of, I realized what the house represented: a void. It was a void I was trying to fill as I was so unhappy with myself. I almost came to resent the house."

Laurie was ready to sell the home sooner than they did, but she knew that her husband loved it. Her heart wasn't in the house, but because he's the thinker, she needed to show him that the house didn't make sense. She showed him the time and money that it was costing them, and the numbers didn't lie. They decided that selling the home would support Laurie in being a stay at home mom and coach. And they decided that the proceeds from the sale would allow a financial cushion for her husband to take a job in the city, travelling less and earning less money.

Without a tear, they sold the dream house. They have now moved into a much smaller home. Laurie says they've shaved decades off their mortgage and have also shaved six hours off of their daily travel time between the two of them. Their new house feels like a home. She shares proudly that they're happier with less. Laurie says, "I realize now what good is a dream home if you never get to dream in it?"

Now Laurie is truly living her dream life. She's a coach and a stay-at-home mom, and her husband is a crane operator. Laurie says that she believes she's been on a journey of becoming the person she was always meant to be. She says that she's always loved sports. She actually left university two years into her science degree, thinking that she would change her focus to become a middle school gym teacher. A summer job with the government that was supposed to last four months turned into a 15-year career, all the way up into a management position. Laurie has now released the "golden handcuffs" of her government work, to be someone who inspires, empowers, and models a true lifestyle shift.

KARA DERINGER

www.karaderinger.com

www.peopleforpeople.ca

Annual People for People Conference
Edmonton, AB, Canada

48270572R00137

Made in the USA
Charleston, SC
29 October 2015